Drawings by
Benjamin West

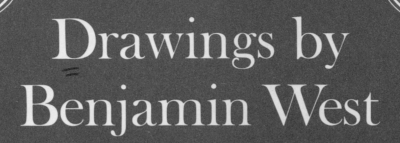

Drawings by Benjamin West

and his son
Raphael Lamar West

by Ruth S. Kraemer

DAVID R. GODINE
&
THE PIERPONT MORGAN LIBRARY

1975

COPYRIGHT © 1975 BY THE PIERPONT MORGAN LIBRARY
29 EAST 36 STREET, NEW YORK, N.Y. 10016
PRINTED IN THE UNITED STATES OF AMERICA
LIBRARY OF CONGRESS CATALOGUE CARD NUMBER 75–7300
ISBN 87598–050–3

Table of Contents

Introduction

THIS BOOK PRESENTS the largest single collection of drawings by
Benjamin West now known; there is also a substantial group of drawings by
his son Raphael Lamar West. Benjamin West's drawings in the collection at
The Pierpont Morgan Library range in time from his earliest finished drawing
which survives (1757) to a sketch for *Peter's Denial of Christ* which is inscribed "the
last design by Benj.ⁿ West 1819." It may well be his last drawing; West died on 11
March 1820. With one or two exceptions, each of the more than two hundred fifty
drawings in this volume is discussed for the first time.

Benjamin West was born on 10 October 1738, the son of the keeper of an inn ten
miles west of Philadelphia. By the time West was eight he was regarded as a prod-
igy. His ability to draw, and later to paint, astounded his family and friends and,
before long, the most cultivated men of Philadelphia, western Pennsylvania, and
then New York. For nearly two hundred years West has been regarded as an un-
taught child of nature with spontaneous genius; he is supposed to have received his
first colors from the Indians. But in the last few decades scholars have pointed out
the romantic distortions in these stories and West's fortunate association with many
of the best minds in the Colonies and with a remarkable, though largely unknown,
American painter, William Williams. Yet we are still only beginning to recognize
the nature and the accomplishment of West's work and his true contribution to the
history of art.

This volume opens with a large finished drawing, *Rebecca at the Well*, inscribed by
the artist: "One of the first attempts at historical composition by Benjⁿ West while
in Philadelphia 1757." A sketchbook from his youth and earlier paintings by him
survive: the paintings are naive though promising landscapes and a few portraits
which are really folk art but less formal and more subtle than those of most of his
contemporary American artists. There is also one historical painting, *The Death of
Socrates*, painted about 1756, during his stay in Lancaster, Pennsylvania.

Rebecca at the Well, like *The Death of Socrates*, and also like some of the early works
of Feke and Copley, must have been based on an engraving: prints and book illustrations were the primary source of European art and of historical subjects for our
first American painters. The derivative nature of West's two early historical works
is obvious, but both are landmarks in the history of American art, and of world art.
When West left America in 1760 for Italy and then England, he had already created
the first images of a new form of painting and drawing which he soon established

abroad as a challenge to the "high art" of France and Italy. As Professor James Flexner has written in a most important essay on "Benjamin West's American Neo-Classicism": "before he saw Italy or Winckelmann, West had painted a neo-classical picture in the backwoods metropolis of Lancaster."

Rebecca at the Well is even more significant in establishing West's innovative genius, for it displays far more skill in its composition than the historical painting he had done a year earlier. This is the only American drawing by West in this collection; it is by far the most important one to have survived. In his American years West was celebrated for his skill in portraiture, but in Italy, where he was received with adulation, West turned toward more literary subjects and was quickly recognized as the "American Raphael." The second drawing here gives evidence of direct copying of ancient reliefs which later served as models for the composition of such pictures as *Agrippina with the Ashes of Germanicus* (1768). The few paintings which are known from the Roman period (1760–63) show West moving closer and closer to a sculpturesque neo-classical style.

Drawings from his early years in London (after August 1763) reveal the evolution of this new style which he more than any other artist made famous. The sketches of historical subjects have a freshness and a spontaneity which are not to be found in his paintings, except occasionally in the small oil sketches. In these first impressions he has the originality of his earliest American work: the drawings are not, for the most part, so self-consciously Italianate and grandiose as the paintings, which created a furor in London, first in the exhibitions of the Society of Artists and then, after 1768, at the Royal Academy, of which he was a founding member. If his paintings seem for us to be frequently arid, with a hard, dull line, these drawings are nervous; they are simple rather than falsely sublime, and gentle rather than overly sentimental and pathetic.

Shown here are preliminary sketches for many of his most famous historical, religious, and literary paintings and designs of the next decades: the altarpiece for Trinity College, Cambridge; the series of huge paintings for the King's Chapel at Windsor; the designs of both the great east window and the altar painting for St. George's Chapel, Windsor; the designs for the windows at Fonthill Abbey; paintings like *Hagar and Ishmael*, *The Raising of Lazarus*, *Christ Healing the Sick in the Temple*, *Death on a Pale Horse* and *Destruction of the Beast and the False Prophet*, *Thetis Bringing the Armor to Achilles*, *The Bard*, *Oliver Cromwell Dissolving the Long Parliament*, *The Death of the Earl of Chatham*, *The Battle of La Hogue*, and *The Death of Nelson*. Many of these drawings reveal the establishment of West's own monumental style; they show him creating a kind of history painting which was more realistic and direct, more contemporaneous, than England and Europe had previously known. West's realism, like that of Copley, as introduced into historical subjects, rejuvenated the classical forms.

If West was a creator of neo-classical art and realistic history painting, he was also a precursor of romantic ideas in art. His romanticism is revealed not so much in the finished drawings (or in his paintings) as in these immediate sketches: here we find new and vigorous concepts of heroism and death, of horror and terror, and we discover new views of nature. Sketching from nature kept West from mannerism and pomposity in most of his drawing; as a result, the sketches of animals, trees, landscapes are outstanding examples of early romantic modes of art. From the 1780's on West drew in Windsor Great Park and Little Park, and was fascinated by ancient blasted trees, with only a few branches of leaves left on the gnarled and twisted stumps. Herne's Oak at Windsor, made famous in *The Merry Wives of Windsor*, especially attracted him and he drew it again and again. For the next forty or fifty years, to the time of John Linnell and George Richmond, and beyond, the parks at Windsor, and the ancient trees, would captivate English artists. In this way, as in so many others, we can see that in these drawings Benjamin West established new subjects for art and new ways of looking at these subjects.

For most of us today, West's achievement is hard to measure in his paintings. As a consequence he is not so well known nor admired as Copley (his exact contemporary), or Stuart or Trumbull, perhaps even as Charles Willson Peale. Their works and life have been much more fully studied. But in his own time West was considered by both Americans and Englishmen to be the leading artist of his age. There was little doubt about his succeeding Sir Joshua Reynolds as the second President of the Royal Academy, or being chosen as Surveyor of the King's Paintings (he held both positions from 1791 to his death in 1820). He was buried beside Sir Joshua in St. Paul's Cathedral. His career was undoubtedly the most successful of any American painter until recent years, perhaps the most successful ever.

Today we can perhaps more easily recognize his importance as a teacher. He taught almost every British painter in the last quarter of the eighteenth century and the first decades of the nineteenth. He was among the first to recognize the genius of Blake, Turner, and Constable. Above all he taught the Americans: those named above as his best-known contemporaries, with others like Pratt, Allston, Morse, Earle, Sully, Rembrandt Peale, and many more. As Professor Flexner has written, "he was incontrovertibly the father of American painting."

On the eve of our bicentennial year, it seems to us at the Morgan Library that it is appropriate to salute the father of American painting with this book and the exhibition (May–July 1975) of his drawings. There have previously been few opportunities to see more than a handful of his drawings at one time. In 1968 the Bernard Black Gallery in New York held an exhibition of thirty-six drawings by West. His virtuosity in drawing was then widely remarked for the first time. Now we present a far larger and more significant body of his work, showing every kind of subject, every kind of technique—from the rustic and natural, to the Italianate, to those later drawings influenced by Dutch or Flemish artists. The drawings illustrated here show the range of penwork from light and delicate to heavy and broad. They show the steps in the growth of a neo-classical, and a romantic artist. We must not forget that as a child his talent was first recognized in his drawings, and in his drawings we shall finally see the most distinctive marks of his originality as an artist.

This volume, also for the first time, makes a comprehensive effort to relate West's drawings to his total *oeuvre*. Mrs. Ruth S. Kraemer has spent several years in the study of these and hundreds of other drawings by West and has established that many of them are preliminary sketches for major paintings or designs for glass although a large number of these have today disappeared. She has also endeavored to separate West's drawings from those of his two sons, and this is often a most difficult task. What emerges from her work is by far the most detailed study of West that has so far been presented. We are all very much in Mrs. Kraemer's debt for her devotion, and for her most impressive analysis of West's art.

This collection of drawings was acquired by The Pierpont Morgan Library in 1970. It was purchased from a New York dealer in art as the gift of Mrs. Robert H. Charles. The Library had immediately realized the importance of keeping the drawings together as a group and Mrs. Charles responded to this opportunity by making the purchase of the entire collection possible; we are deeply grateful to her. All of the drawings came from direct descendants of Benjamin West: the major part of the collection from Harry Margary, who is the great-grandson of Maria West, the daughter of Raphael Lamar West (and granddaughter of Benjamin); she had married Thomas George Margary. Drawing Nos. 2, 20, and 37 in this volume were originally in the collection of Mrs. Claire Francis (sold at Christie's on 14 March 1967), also a descendant of Benjamin West.

Miss Felice Stampfle, Curator of Drawings and Prints, has taken a great interest in this collection and has supervised all of the work in connection with it, this publication, and the exhibition. The last three years have been spent in conserving the drawings (much work was required, and this was done in our conservation laboratory, chiefly by Mrs. Patricia Reyes), cataloguing and classifying them, building up an archive of photographs and printed material concerning West's life and work, and preparing this volume for the press. The photographs for this volume were taken at the Library by the head of the photographic department, Charles Passela.

The Library is most grateful to the National Endowment for the Arts in Washington, D.C., a Federal agency, for a generous grant in support of the publication of this volume and the exhibition.

Charles Ryskamp
DIRECTOR

Acknowledgments

I AM DEEPLY INDEBTED to Miss Felice Stampfle, Curator of Drawings, who supervised this project and who was always ready with expert advice and helpful suggestions. Without her faithful assistance and constant encouragement, the formidable task of cataloguing over two hundred fifty drawings could not have been accomplished. Thanks are due to the Library for providing the funds for travel and the acquisition of a photographic archive, and to members of the staff for their help, especially to Mrs. Cara D. Denison, the Associate Curator of Drawings, and Mr. Alexander Jensen Yow, the Conservator. I am most grateful to Linda Rashman, secretarial assistant in the Department of Drawings, who typed the manuscript and assisted in many ways with the preparation of the catalogue.

Professor Helmut von Erffa generously provided me with much valuable information during two meetings in 1972 when I started work on this catalogue. I should also like to thank the curators of the collections at many museums who facilitated the study of the West material under their care, especially Jane Rittenhouse, Director of the Friends Historical Library, and Professor Robert Walker, both at Swarthmore College, and Andrew Wilton, Assistant Keeper, Department of Prints and Drawings at the British Museum. I also owe a debt of gratitude to the following collectors and public institutions that were especially helpful in my research and graciously granted permission to publish their material in this catalogue: an anonymous private collector; the Archives of American Art, New York; the Ashmolean Museum, Oxford; the Baltimore Museum of Art; the Boston Museum of Fine Arts; the Delaware Art Museum, Wilmington, Delaware; the Detroit Institute of Arts; Lord Egremont, Petworth House, Sussex; the Folger Shakespeare Library, Washington, D.C.; the Frick Art Reference Library, New York; the Henry E. Huntington Library and Art Gallery, San Marino, California; the Historical Society of Pennsylvania, Philadelphia; the Library of Congress, Washington, D.C.; Mr. and Mrs. Paul Mellon, Upperville, Virginia; the Metropolitan Museum of Art, New York; Sir Oliver Millar, Surveyor of the Queen's Pictures, London; the Minneapolis Institute of Arts; the Montclair Art Museum; Museo de Arte de Ponce, Puerto Rico; the National Gallery of Art, Washington, D.C.; the New Britain Museum of Art; the New-York Historical Society; the New York Public Library; the Art Gallery of Ontario, Toronto, Canada; the Philadelphia Museum of Art; the Royal Academy of Arts, London; the Royal Library, Windsor Castle; Rutgers University Library and Art Gallery, New Brunswick, New Jersey; the Tate Gallery, London;

the Toledo Museum of Art; the Vassar College Art Gallery, Poughkeepsie, New York; the Victoria & Albert Museum, London; the Whitworth Art Gallery, Manchester, England; the Witt Library, Courtauld Institute of Art, University of London.

I also gratefully acknowledge the help of Messrs. Evelyn Joll and Clovis Whitfield of Thos. Agnew & Sons, Ltd., London; Mr. Henry D. Hill of the Berry-Hill Galleries, Inc., New York; Mr. Bernard Black of the Black-Nadeau Gallery, Monte Carlo; Mr. Francis Russell of Christie, Manson & Woods Ltd., London; Mr. S. A. Leger of the Leger Galleries Ltd., London; Mr. William Drummond of the Sabin Galleries, London; and the staffs of the Hirschl & Adler, Kennedy, and Knoedler Galleries in New York.

R. S. K.

Catalogue

Works Cited in Abbreviated Form

Bernard Black Gallery
Exhibition Catalogue
: *A Benjamin West Portfolio, Drawings and Studies*, catalogue by E. Maurice Bloch, Bernard Black Gallery, New York, 14 May – 1 June 1968.

Churchill
: W. A. Churchill, *Watermarks in Paper in Holland, England, France, etc. in the XVII and XVIII Centuries and Their Interconnection*, Amsterdam, 1935.

Evans, *West*
: Grose Evans, *Benjamin West and the Taste of His Times*, Carbondale, Illinois, 1959.

Farington Diary
: Joseph Farington, R.A., *The Farington Diary*, ed. by James Greig, 8 vols., London, 1923–28.

Galt, *Life*
: John Galt, *The Life of Benjamin West (1816–1820)*, a facsimile reproduction with an introduction by Nathalia Wright, Scholars' Facsimiles & Reprints, Gainesville, Florida, 1960.

Galt, *Life*, folio ed.
: John Galt, *The Life, Studies, and Works of Benjamin West, Esq.*, 7 vols., folio edition, London, 1820 (copy at Historical Society of Pennsylvania, Philadelphia).

Heawood
: Edward Heawood, *Watermarks, Mainly of the 17th and 18th Centuries*, Hilversum, Holland, 1950.

George Robins sale
catalogue of 1829
: *A Catalogue Raisonné of the unequalled collection of Historical Pictures, and other compositions, the works of the revered and highly-gifted painter, the late Benjamin West, Esq . . .* which will be sold by auction by Mr. George Robins . . . on Friday, Saturday, & Monday, May 22ᵈ, 23ᵈ, & 25ᵗʰ, 1829, in Lots.

Royal Academy exhibitions
of West paintings
: Algernon Graves, *The Royal Academy of Arts, A Complete Dictionary of Contributors and their work from its foundation in 1769 to 1904*, vol. 4, London, 1905 (reprint edition, 1970).

1839 sale catalogue of
West drawings
: *Catalogue of One Hundred and Twenty Original Drawings, by the late Benjamin West, Esq. . . .* which will be sold by auction by Mr. S. Leigh Sotheby, . . . on Saturday, the 1st of June, 1839.

*Supplement to
La Belle Assemblée*
: "A Correct Catalogue of the Works of Benjamin West, Esq.," *Supplement to La Belle Assemblée or, Bell's Court and Fashionable Magazine*, IV, 1 July 1808, pp. 13–20.

RELIGIOUS, HISTORICAL, AND MYTHOLOGICAL SUBJECTS

I

Rebecca at the Well

1970.11:1   PLATE I

Point of brush, black wash over black chalk on light-brown paper, some passages outlined with pen and black ink, on two sheets of paper pasted together. 13 5/16 x 20 5/8 inches (339 x 523 mm.). Inscribed by the artist in pen and brown ink: *One of the first attempts at historical composition by Benjn West. while in Philadelphia 1757.* Verso: Portrait of a gentleman, and sketch of a group of women, perhaps for the composition on recto, in black chalk. Watermark: None.

This drawing is of great significance as it represents, in the artist's own words, one of his first ventures into the field of historical painting. Only one other example of this very early period has survived, *The Death of Socrates*, the painting which West executed about 1756 during his stay in Lancaster, Pennsylvania, at the suggestion of William Henry, the revolutionary patriot and master gun-smith (see Ann C. Van Devanter, "Benjamin West's Death of Socrates," *Antiques*, CIV, September 1973, pp. 436–39). This painting, which was rediscovered by James Thomas Flexner in 1952, is now in the collection of Mrs. Thomas H. A. Stites, Nazareth, Pennsylvania. Flexner in his essay "Benjamin West's American Neo-Classicism" (*The New-York Historical Society Quarterly*, XXXVI, 1952, pp. 5–34) pointed out that, as a model for the composition, West used the frontispiece in Volume IV of Charles Rollin's *Ancient History*, an engraving by Jacques Philippe Le Bas after a drawing by Hubert François Gravelot. Galt (*Life*, I, p. 21) states that West as a boy was given six engravings by Grevling (presumably Gravelot) by a relative from Philadelphia, and it is perhaps in Gravelot's *oeuvre* or among similar book illustrations that one may discover the model West used for the Morgan Library's drawing *Rebecca at the Well*. That West was interested at this time in biblical or even apocryphal stories is demonstrated by the present drawing as well as by Galt who notes that West executed a *Trial of Susannah* for a patron named Cox and that "in point of composition, Mr. West is of opinion that the Trial of Susannah was superior to the Death of Socrates" (*Life*, I, pp. 72–74).

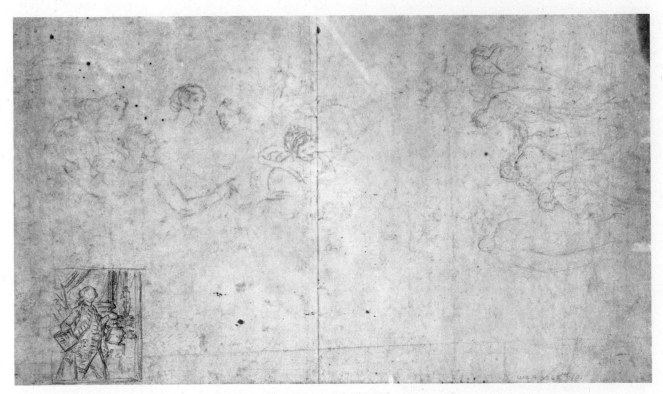

Fig. 1   Portrait of a Gentleman, and Compositional Sketch (Verso of Plate 1).

[3]

A comparison between *Rebecca at the Well* and the *Death of Socrates* (see Pl. 1 and G. Evans, *West*, pl. 13) reveals considerable artistic development in the former, in the composition as a whole, and in the less rigid and more spacious disposition of the figures themselves, which have gained in volume and articulation. This holds true even if one bears in mind that the painting *The Death of Socrates* has sustained extensive losses and overpainting in the past and has only recently been cleaned and restored.

West painted another version of the Rebecca story about nine years later in England. The records of the Royal Academy mention *Isaac's Servant Tying the Bracelet on Rebecca's Arm* in 1776 (no. 319), which possibly is the picture executed for Lord Buckinghamshire (*Supplement to La Belle Assemblée*, p. 16). There also was a drawing of the subject in black chalk in the 1839 sale of West drawings (Sotheby, *Catalogue of One Hundred and Twenty Original Drawings by the late Benjamin West, Esq.*, 1 June 1839, p. 3, Lot 11). In the Morgan Library's drawing Isaac's servant appears to present a bracelet or a piece of jewelry to Rebecca, but does not fasten the bracelet to her arm. A drawing at the Boston Museum of Fine Arts (Acc. No. 42.600) perhaps shows this later version of the subject.

The preliminary sketch for a portrait on the verso of the Morgan Library's drawing (Fig. 1) is very close to the drawings in West's early sketchbook at the Historical Society of Pennsylvania, Philadelphia (AM 186). It dates back to the period when the young artist earned his livelihood by portraying members of colonial Philadelphia society before setting out on his trip to Italy in 1760. The sketch shows a gentleman in a splendid eighteenth-century costume standing in front of a column, his right hand at his hip, his three-cornered hat tucked under his left arm. There is a drapery at the upper left and a small statue at the upper right, perhaps indicating the sitter's connection with the arts.

Fig. 2   Procession of Romans after the Ara Pacis.
Philadelphia, Philadelphia Museum of Art, Given by The Robert L. McNeil, Jr., Trusts.

2

Procession of Romans after the Ara Pacis, Rome

1970.11:164   PLATE 2

Black chalk heightened with white on gray paper. Stains of black and red ink at lower right. 8 x 10½ inches (202 x 268 mm.). Verso: Sketch of robed figure in black chalk. Watermark: Fragment of fleur-de-lis inscribed in circle.

This drawing and another at the Philadelphia Museum of Art (67.153.1; graphite, 8 x 10½ inches. Fig. 2) are exact copies of the reliefs from the Ara Pacis in Rome. The former shows part of the procession on the north side of the altar, the latter that on the south side (cf. Giuseppe Moretti, *The Ara Pacis Augustae*, Rome, n.d., pp. 39 and 36). Both drawings are so fresh and true that they appear to have been made in front of the marble reliefs and not copied from a publication of antique sculpture.

It has been noted that the painting *Agrippina Landing at Brundisium with the Ashes of Germanicus* shows in the procession of Roman women a certain reflection of the Ara Pacis reliefs and it has been assumed that West must have known the reliefs themselves (cf. Allen Staley, "The Landing of Agrippina at Brundisium with the Ashes of Germanicus," *Bulletin, Philadelphia Museum of Art*, LXI, 1965–66, pp. 10–19). The New York and Philadelphia drawings are direct evidence for such knowledge. West possibly saw the reliefs in Rome or perhaps in Florence where some sections of the frieze could be seen in the Uffizi Gallery at the time he was in Italy, 1760–63.

Agrippina Landing at Brundisium with the Ashes of Germanicus, which assured West a place among the first European artists introducing the neo-classical style, perhaps just for this reason, also brought about a turning-point in his career. The painting was commissioned by Dr. Robert Drummond, Archbishop of York, one of West's early patrons in England, and when it was shown to the King, it impressed him so much that he immediately ordered West to paint another subject from Roman history, *The Departure of Regulus*, dated 1769, now at Kensington Palace. It was the interest this painting aroused in the King that led to the long period of royal patronage and assured the artist a carefree, comfortable existence.

West exhibited two paintings of the subject at the Society of Artists in 1768 (nos. 175 and 120). Today, three versions are known: a large painting at the Yale University Art Gallery; one in the possession of the Earl of Exeter at Burghley House, Northamptonshire; and a small oil sketch signed and dated 1766, at the Philadelphia Museum of Art, possibly the original oil sketch for Yale's large painting.

3

A Group of Four Women

1970.11:94

Black chalk. 8⅞ x 11¾ inches (227 x 299 mm.). Inscribed in pen and brown ink: *Lot 73/2 Titiano*. Watermark: None.

This delicate drawing of women in flowing draperies has so far eluded any attempt to connect it with one of West's paintings. It is undoubtedly an early drawing, as a comparison with a few of West's figures of women in his paintings of about 1766–68 confirms. Suffice it to mention the figure of Iphigenia in the painting *Orestes and Pylades* of 1766 at the Tate Gallery, London, who wears a costume similar to that of the figure at the extreme right in the Morgan drawing. Her cloak is draped around her body in like fashion, with a piece of the cloth falling over her arm. The same graceful movement of the body can be observed in the young woman at the extreme right in the preparatory drawing for *Jacob Blessing Joseph's Two Sons Ephraim and Manasseh*, the painting now at the Allen Art Museum, Oberlin, Ohio. This drawing, formerly on the New York art market, is signed and dated *B. West 1768* (Fig. 3). There the woman is seen from the back at the same angle as in the Library's drawing.

4

Drapery Study for a Seated Woman

1970.11:166

Black chalk on blue-gray paper. 18⅞ x 11⅞ inches (480 x 303 mm.). Watermark: None.

Fig. 3 Jacob Blessing Joseph's Two Sons Ephraim and Manasseh.
Formerly New York Art Market.

This drawing is possibly a preliminary study for Agrippina's garment in the painting *Agrippina and Her Children Mourning over the Ashes of Germanicus* of 1773 at the John and Mable Ringling Museum of Art, Sarasota, Florida (canvas, 80 x 56½ inches). The Library's study, however, is closer to the preparatory drawing for the same painting at the Historical Society of Pennsylvania, Philadelphia (Vol. I of West drawings, p. 13; black chalk, 12⅝ x 9¾ inches), which is signed and dated *B. West 1771* (G. Evans, *West*, pls. 24 and 25). In the Philadelphia drawing as in the Morgan sheet, the cloth falls in a curve over Agrippina's knees down to her feet. In the painting the fall of the drapery is not as clearly visible because Agrippina's child, depicted as a young boy, leans against his mother's knees while in the Philadelphia drawing he is represented as a baby on her lap.

5

The Return of the Prodigal Son (?)
1970.11:13

Red chalk on gray paper. 6⅜ x 6⅜ inches (162 x 162 mm.). Verso: Two rough sketches in red chalk. Watermark: J. Whatman.

The red chalk of this study is a medium rarely used by West. Another instance of its use is *In the Nursery*, the drawing signed and dated *B. West 1784* in the British Museum (1887-6-13-3). West painted two pictures of *The Return of the Prodigal Son*: one was exhibited at the Royal Academy in 1771 (no. 215), the other in 1773 (no. 307; see A. Ten Eyck Gardner and Stuart Feld, *American Paintings, A Catalogue of the Collection of the Metropolitan Museum of Art*, I, 1965, pp. 26–27). George Robins' sale catalogue of 1829 lists as Lot 16 on page 8 a small painting of the subject (11 x 12 inches) in which "the fond father is about to wrap his penitent, wretched son, in his own mantle." This description does not fit the Morgan Library's drawing nor a painting in the Metropolitan Museum attributed to West in the 1965 catalogue of the American paintings, but now questioned as his work. The Morgan Library's drawing differs in many respects from the painting, especially in the rustic appearance of the old man with his straggly hair and beard, and tattered clothes. Could he perhaps be interpreted as Orestes' old servant greeting the returning stranger? Yet the relationship of the two figures in the drawing seems to have a certain affinity with the way they are combined in the painting. On the other hand, again, the head in profile, at the lower right, is puzzling in connection with the parable of the Prodigal Son, and a different interpretation of the subject of the drawing may be called for.

6

The Infant St. John
1970.11:190   PLATE 3

Graphite on brown paper. Squared for transfer and traced with the stylus. 15 13/16 x 11 3/4 inches (402 x 300 mm.). Horizontal crease in center; irregular margins; several small stains. Verso: Rubbed with red chalk. Watermark: None.

This drawing, which has been prepared for transfer to either canvas or plate or both, can undoubtedly be connected with Lot 22 of George Robins' sale catalogue of 1829 which is described as "a pleasing allegory, wherein the infant Baptist is fondling a lamb...." Its measurements, 1 foot 5 1/2 inches high by 1 foot 1 inch wide, differ by about one inch in either direction from those of the drawing. According to a notation in the margin of the Frick Library's copy of the 1829 sale catalogue, the picture was acquired for thirty-nine guineas by Dunlap through the good offices of a solicitor called Dubois. The buyer was perhaps West's one-time pupil William Dunlap, the American painter and author of the *History of . . . Arts of Design in the United States* of 1834, who was living in America at the time of the sale. The fate of the painting has not been ascertained.

The composition in this drawing has been conceived under the influence of the Italian masters such as Raphael, Leonardo, or Del Sarto. It also was a favorite theme of Murillo. The type of the young St. John with his pretty features, curly hair, and smooth skin may be compared with Agrippina's child in West's painting *Agrippina and Her Children Mourning over the Ashes of Germanicus* of 1773 at the John and Mable Ringling Museum of Art, Sarasota, Florida (cf. G. Evans, *West*, pl. 25). The drawing may originate from about this time.

7

The Death of Epaminondas (?)
1970.11:76   PLATE 4

Black chalk. 3 13/16 x 5 3/8 inches (97 x 136 mm.). Watermark: None.

This small sketch may have been made in preparation for *The Death of Epaminondas*, one of the pictures which West executed for the King's apartment at Queen's House or Buckingham House, the royal residence on the site now occupied by Buckingham Palace. The painting, which is now at Kensington Palace, is signed and dated *B. West/ 1773* (see Oliver Millar, *The Later Georgian Pictures in the Collection of Her Majesty the Queen*, London, 1969, no. 1156, pl. 123); it is mentioned in Galt's catalogue of West's works (*Life*, II, p. 207) and was exhibited at the Royal Academy in 1773 (no. 304). In the drawing, the wounded hero of the Battle of Mantinea (362 B.C.) is seen lying on the ground, his head propped up against the man seated behind him. The standing soldier with the plumed helmet and the warrior approaching with Epaminondas' shield on the left also appear in the painting. Epaminondas, however, is represented in the painting in a sitting position with part of the spear protruding from his chest. According to the legend, he did not want the point of the spear removed, which would result in his death, until he knew that his shield had been saved. The tent in the drawing is also different from that in the painting; it seems rather to be a piece of drapery used as a makeshift shelter for the dying man.

Another drawing, at the Kennedy Galleries in New York (pencil, 13 x 18 inches), may be a preparatory sketch for the same composition. Here, however, the scene takes place under palm trees in a mountain landscape with the Theban army's tents visible in the background, not in front of a large tent as in the painting.

8

Family Group
1970.11:137

Oval design in black chalk; lines traced with stylus. 2 9/16 x 1 7/8 inches (65 x 49 mm.). Laid down. Border of gray wash on old mat. Watermark: None.

This small sketch of the members of a family surrounding a sick youth was perhaps intended for book illustration, as the design has been traced for transfer. It calls to mind the painting *The Golden Age* of 1776 at the Tate Gallery which, in a horizontal oval, depicts a mother and child and, in the distance on the right, near an open door, an elderly couple. (It has been surmised that the young woman dressed in white is a portrait of West's wife and the baby their infant son; however, in 1776, their second son, Benjamin Jr., would have been four years old.)

9

Hagar and Ishmael
1970.11:202   PLATE 4

Black chalk. 5 1/8 x 3 11/16 inches (131 x 94 mm.). Watermark: None.

This drawing may be a first idea for West's painting *Hagar and Ishmael*, now at the Metropolitan Museum of Art, New York (oil on canvas, 76 x 54 1/2 inches), which is signed and dated at lower right *B. West/1776*, at lower left *B. West 1803*. As in the case of the version of the *Battle of La Hogue*, also now at the Metropolitan Museum of Art, New York, West was in the habit of retouching or repainting certain portions of his paintings long after their completion, sometimes after an interval of over twenty-five years. The Metropolitan Museum's picture was painted for Thomas Dawson, Lord Cremorne, an Irish nobleman (1725–1813), but West later regained possession of it and, after making some changes, sent it to the Royal Academy for exhibition in 1803. It was this picture which caused a bitter controversy between the artist and the council of members of the Royal Academy as it was against the rules to submit one and the same picture twice, and the original version had been exhibited in 1776 (see A. Ten Eyck Gardner and Stuart P. Feld, *American Paintings, A Catalogue of the Collection of the Metropolitan Museum of Art*, I, 1965, pp. 28–29).

There is a fine preparatory drawing for the above painting at the Victoria and Albert Museum (Acc. No. 203-1890; black and white chalk, and white, blue, and red body color, on gray paper, 12 1/8 x 8 7/8 inches. Fig. 4). It is signed and dated *B. West.1776* and shows the earlier state of the painting. Two drawings of Hagar and Ishmael are mentioned in C. Smart's catalogue *West's Gallery / Newman Street*, London, 1823, as being exhibited in the Room of Drawings (pp. 3–4, nos. 10 and 48); one of these was undoubtedly the highly finished drawing at the Victoria and Albert Museum.

In the Morgan Library's drawing Hagar is supporting the limp body of her young child stretched out across her lap; Ishmael in the Victoria and Albert Museum's drawing, as well as in the painting, appears to be an older boy. In the Library's drawing, Hagar, an expression of fear on her face, gestures in helplessness and despair as she looks up at the angel appearing in the clouds. His head is seen in profile in contrast to that in the painting but the position of his arms and hands is similar. There is a landscape with mountains visible through the trees, which were omitted in both the finished drawing and the painting. Two further drawings of the subject exist: one large finished sheet (no. 2310, pen and brown ink and blue wash, 17 1/2 x 20 1/4 inches) signed and dated *B. West 1788*, at the Addison Gallery of American Art, and another sketch (black crayon, 6 3/8 x 8 3/8 inches) which was included in the 1968 exhibition at the Bernard Black Gallery, New York (*A Benjamin West Portfolio*, no. 10). These two drawings show horizontal compositions in contrast to the vertical ones discussed and may possibly be later conceptions of the same theme.

The Morgan Library's drawing shows some resemblance in composition with the charming pen sketch of a mother and child, signed and dated *B. West 1783*, at the British Museum (1871.6-10-761; 7 x 4 13/16 inches). The type of the child as well as his position on the mother's lap, with one arm dangling between her legs, recalls the group in the Morgan drawing.

Fig. 4   Hagar and Ishmael.
London, Victoria & Albert Museum, Crown Copyright.

Fig. 5   W. BYRNE. Thalia. Engraving.
London, British Museum.

10

Thalia and a Male Nude
The figure of Thalia is a sketch for the title page of Volume VII of *The New English Theatre*, London, 1777.

1970.11:204   PLATE 5

Pen and brown ink. 4⅜ x 7¾ inches (111 x 196 mm.). Irregular upper margin. Watermark: Crown, fragment of coat-of-arms (close to Heawood 446–47).

The charming girl seated in the clouds and holding a mask represents Thalia, the muse of comedy. She is undoubtedly a first sketch for the figure who appears in a frontal pose, in reversed direction, on the engraved title page of Volume VII of *The New English Theatre*, a set of twelve volumes published in 1776–77, which contains the most valuable plays that had been acted on the London stage. In the engraving Thalia is accompanied by a cherub blowing a small trumpet and beating a tambourine, and four others playing hot cockles in the clouds.

The impression of the engraving at the British Museum (43-5-13-42; 6¾ x 4½ inches. Fig. 5) is signed *B. West invt* and *W. Byrne sculpt*. William Byrne is known to have collaborated with the well-known engraver Francesco Bartolozzi, so it is not surprising to find this engraving listed in Calabi's catalogue of Bartolozzi's works as no. 1792 on page 451 (A. Calabi, *Francesco Bartolozzi, Catalogue des Estampes*, Milan, 1928).

Two other West drawings for the same publication represent *Melpomene*, the tragic muse, Historical Society of Pennsylvania (Galt, *Life*, folio ed., I,

p. 123, and v, p. 50, interleaved). The sketch initialed *BW* (pen and brown ink, 4¾ x 6⁹⁄₁₆ inches) shows only the figure of the muse, but the drawing signed and dated *B. West 1776* (pen and brown ink and brown wash, 6 x 3⅜ inches) is the complete design for the title page of Volume x of *The New English Theatre* (A. Calabi, *op. cit.*, p. 451, no. 1793). It depicts the tragic muse holding a chalice and a dagger, with two weeping putti at her side, as she is seen floating above a scene of combat and a burning building. This sketch may be Lot 31 "The Tragic Muse. Outline in pen and washed with bistre" in the 1839 sale catalogue of Benjamin West's drawings.

I I

Dancing Girl with a Veil
1970.11:220

Pen and brown ink over black chalk. 5⅛ x 3¾ inches (131 x 96 mm.). Laid down. Border on old mat executed in gray wash. Signed in black chalk at lower right: *B. West*. Watermark: None.

This charming pen sketch shows a girl in a high-waisted, clinging gown, holding a large, fluttering veil and taking some tentative dance steps. The clouds around her are lightly indicated in black chalk. This figure, composed within the vertical format of Thalia and Melpomene (Cat. No. 10) can perhaps be identified with Terpsichore, the muse of the dance, and may have been drawn for the title page of another volume in *The New English Theatre* series.

I 2

Young Woman Holding Up a Bow with Both Hands
1970.11:169

Black chalk, heightened with white, on blue-gray paper. 7⅛ x 5¹¹⁄₁₆ inches (184 x 144 mm.). Verso: Faint sketch in black chalk for a female portrait. Watermark: None.

Although executed in a different medium, this wavy-haired figure in a high-waisted, transparent gown, seated in a graceful pose within what appears to be a rectangular niche, seems to have been conceived in a vein similar to Thalia (see No. 10) and may also have been intended by the artist for book illustration or a related purpose.

I 3

St. Michael and the Dragon
Study for the painting at Trinity College, Cambridge, England.
1970.11:215   PLATES 6 AND 7

Black chalk. 5¹¹⁄₁₆ x 3 inches (145 x 75 mm.). Verso: Study in black chalk for *The Raising of Lazarus*. Watermark: Pro Patria.

The painting *St. Michael and the Dragon* (executed in oil on canvas, 172 x 80 inches) is signed and dated *B. West 1777* (Fig. 6). It originally was the altarpiece of the Chapel at Trinity College, but was removed about 1875 and now hangs on the staircase of the college library. The painting was exhibited at the Royal Academy in 1777 (no. 365). The composition of the Morgan drawing and the painting, both of which have an arched top, is very close indeed. The only variation is to be found in the reversed position of the Archangel's legs; also the dragon's tail wound around his human upper body seems narrower.

There are two fine drawings for the Trinity College painting at the Friends Historical Library, Swarthmore College, Swarthmore, Pennsylvania. They are both executed in black chalk, heightened with white, on blue paper; one sheet (P.P. 256; 15¼ x 9½ inches. Fig. 7) shows the figure of St. Michael as well as a sketch of the entire composition, very similar to the Morgan Library's; the other (P.P. 175; 6¾ x 5⅛ inches) represents the figure of the Archangel holding a torch in his right hand and a shield in his left. There is also a smaller painted version of the subject (29½ x 46¼ inches) signed and dated *B. West 1776* in the James H. Ricau collection, Piermont, New York; St. Michael here is holding a thunderbolt instead of the spear in his right hand.

West executed another painting of *St. Michael and the Dragon* for William Beckford in 1797; it is the cartoon executed in oil on canvas (50⅛ x 23½ inches) for a stained-glass window in Fonthill Abbey, now in the Toledo Museum of Art (Acc. No.

points out their relationship to Guido Reni's painting of the Archangel St. Michael in S. Maria della Concezione, Rome, which West may have seen during his visit to Rome in 1760–63.

The sketch on the verso of the Morgan Library's drawing may be a study for *The Raising of Lazarus*, a painting also exhibited at the Royal Academy in 1777 (no. 366). This painting was identified in the catalogue of the West exhibition at Allentown

Fig. 6   St. Michael and the Dragon.
Cambridge, Trinity College, Courtesy of The Master and Fellows.

Fig. 7   St. Michael and the Dragon.
Swarthmore, Pennsylvania, Swarthmore College, Friends Historical Library.

59.33). Compared to the earlier, more static compositions, the action here has become more dramatic by the addition of several fallen angels and numerous serpents, and the fierce expression of the Archangel's face. Millard F. Rogers ("Benjamin West and the Caliph: two paintings for Fonthill Abbey," *Apollo*, 83, June 1966, pp. 420–25) discusses West's several versions of the subject and

Pennsylvania, in 1962 (pp. 54–55, no. 10) with the oil sketch in *grisaille* on canvas (30¼ x 35¼ inches) at the Friends Historical Library, Swarthmore College; it is signed and dated *B. West 1776* and was inscribed by the artist at lower right *Retouched 1814*. The picture was included as Lot 118 in George Robins' sale catalogue of 1829 where it is described as "Painted in chiaro scuro. The original study for the great Altar-piece in Winchester Cathedral." This altarpiece was exhibited at the Royal Academy in 1780 and is now at the Wadsworth Atheneum, Hartford; it was presented to the museum by J. Pierpont Morgan in 1900 (8 feet 5 inches by 10 feet 10 inches; for illustrations, see G. Evans, *West*, pls. 7 and 8). West painted yet another version of *The Raising of Lazarus*, the "finished sketch" exhibited at the Royal Academy in 1791, which may be identical with the painting now at the Glasgow Art Gallery and Museum, Glasgow (oil on paper, mounted on canvas, 28½ x 46 inches), which is signed and dated *B. West 1788*.

The Library's Lazarus sketch differs considerably from the Swarthmore and Hartford paintings. It shows Christ lifting the shroud from Lazarus while a kneeling woman, possibly the dead man's sister Martha, and a group of men witness the miracle. The drawings discussed in the two entries following can perhaps also be connected with the Swarthmore and Hartford paintings.

14

The Raising of Lazarus
1970.11:77

Pen and brown ink. 3 x 4⅜ inches (76 x 111 mm.). Laid down. Ink blot at left center. Watermark: None.

In this sketch the miracle takes place in an arcaded hall or cloister; two of the arches are covered with a drapery, the third opens out into the landscape. Christ, on the left, is removing the shroud from Lazarus who has raised himself from the bier or coffin. The kneeling woman and the group of standing men in robes observed in the preceding drawing can also be seen here.

15

The Raising of Lazarus
1970.11:249   PLATE 7

Black chalk. 4⅝ x 6¾ inches (118 x 172 mm.). Several stains at right center. Watermark: None.

The composition of this drawing is somewhat closer to that of the Swarthmore and Hartford paintings. Although in contrast to the paintings Christ is

placed on the left and Lazarus on the right, and although he raises his left arm in a different gesture as he speaks the words "Lazarus come forth," there are nevertheless similarities in the figure of Lazarus, his bearded face "bound about with a napkin," and the drapery covering the niche where Lazarus' coffin stands. The nude man seated at the right was changed in the paintings to the kneeling figure seen from the back.

16

Chryseis Returned to Her Father Chryses
Study for the painting at the New-York Historical Society (Acc. No. 1865.1).
1970.11:69   PLATE 8

Pen and dark-brown ink on gray paper. 4¾ x 6¹⁵⁄₁₆ inches (121 x 176 mm.). Laid down. Watermark: None.

This spirited pen sketch is probably a first idea for the painting *Chryseis Returned to Her Father* (oil on canvas, 73¼ x 55¼ inches) which is signed and dated *B. West 1777*. This painting and its companion piece *Hector Parting with His Wife and Child at the Scaean Gate* were given to the New-York Historical Society by William H. Webb in 1865. Both early catalogues of West's works, Galt (*Life*, II, p. 225) as well as the *Supplement to La Belle Assemblée* (*op. cit.*, p. 16), mention "The picture of Chryseis returned to her father Chryses." According to the latter, both pictures were in West's house at Windsor in 1808. A small oil sketch of the subject of Chryseis' return was included in George Robins' sale catalogue of 1829 (Lot 178; 16 x 39 inches) and a drawing "Outline, in sepia, and washed with the same" is mentioned in the 1839 sale catalogue of West drawings (Lot 14). The latter may well be the beautiful wash drawing at the Historical Society of Pennsylvania, Philadelphia (Vol. I of West drawings, p. 15; pen, black ink, and brown wash, 8¹³⁄₁₆ x 6¾ inches. Fig. 8), which is very close to the painting at the New-York Historical Society.

The story is taken from Book I of the *Iliad*. When Chryseis, a beautiful captive of the Greeks, became the property of Agamemnon, her father, the priest of Apollo, went to the Greek camp to solicit his daughter's return, but to no avail. He therefore implored the aid of Apollo, who afflicted the conquerors with a plague and thus forced them to return Chryseis.

The composition in the Morgan Library's drawing is inscribed in a horizontal rectangle while in the Philadelphia sheet and in the painting it is changed to a vertical format. Furthermore, the position of the figures has been reversed; Chryseis and her father are on the right and Agamemnon on the left in the Morgan drawing, and vice versa. The temple of Apollo is indicated by two fluted columns in the Morgan drawing; in the Philadelphia sheet the architecture of the temple has been vertically extended, and a portico and ships can be seen in the distance. In the painting the action takes place in front of an arch which corresponds to a similar architectural setting in *Hector Parting with His Wife and Child* (see G. Evans, *West*, p. 1, pl. 28), the companion piece to this picture.

17

Naval Battle
1970.11:64

Black chalk. 3 1/16 x 5 13/16 inches (77 x 147 mm.). Laid down. Brown ink stain in upper right corner. Border on old mat executed in gray wash. Signed in black chalk on mat by the artist at lower right: *B. West*. Inscribed in pen and brown ink on verso: *Alfred Russel Margary from his affecte Grandmother Mrs West 1848*. Watermark: None.

The burning warship enveloped in clouds of smoke and surrounded by a number of small boats may be a first idea for West's historical painting *The Battle of La Hogue* of 1778, now at the National Gallery of Art, Washington, D.C. It is known that in this naval battle off Cape La Hogue near Cherbourg in May 1692, the English under the command of Admiral George Rooke burned the ships of the French fleet. A comparison between the Morgan Library's small sketch and the elaborate compositional drawing for the above painting at the British Museum (1860.6.9.1; pen and brown ink and gray wash on cream-colored paper, 6 7/16 x 9 13/16 inches; signed and dated *B. West 177*[?], last digit rubbed out) suggests, however, that the present drawing may have been no more than a preliminary notation which West later enlarged and developed into a grand and dramatic scheme. Dunlap recorded that when West was preparing

Fig. 8   Chryseis Returned to Her Father Chryses. *Philadelphia, Historical Society of Pennsylvania.*

to paint the *Battle of La Hogue*, "an admiral took him to Spithead, and to give him a lesson on the effect of smoke in a naval engagement, ordered several ships of the fleet to manoeuvre as in action, and fire broadsides, while the painter made notes" (see Gardner and Feld, *American Paintings, A Catalogue of the Collection of the Metropolitan Museum of Art*, I, p. 29).

The affectionate grandmother who inscribed this drawing to her grandson was Maria Siltso West, Raphael West's wife. Alfred Russel Margary was the son of Raphael West's daughter, Maria, and hence the great-grandson of Benjamin West.

18

Sailing Vessel and Longboats
1970.11:121   PLATE 9

Black chalk on cream-colored paper. 15 1/2 x 12 5/8 inches (394 x 321 mm.). Several tears; paper soiled along left and right margins. Watermark: Letters IHS surmounted by cross and the name I Villedary (close to Heawood 2971).

This drawing shows several small boats filled with

men approaching a large vessel, its sails gracefully slack, lying at anchor in a port. Some of the men are seen climbing aboard the big ship from one of the small boats. There are houses visible in the distance on the left, and a walled city and a horse-drawn covered wagon on the right. Two similar longboats were used by West in his historical painting *The Battle of La Hogue* of 1778, now at the National Gallery of Art, Washington, D.C.; moreover, the man standing up in front of one of the boats and pointing with his right arm also appears in this painting. While this slim connection may not be enough to provide even an approximate date for the Morgan Library's drawing, it does appear to be early.

Fig. 9 JEAN-BAPTISTE MICHEL.
William de Albanac Presenting His Three Daughters to Alfred III, King of Mercia.
Engraving.
London, British Museum.

19

Half-Draped Female Nude
Study for the lost painting *William de Albanac Presenting His Three Daughters to Alfred III, King of Mercia*
1970.11:196   PLATE 6

Black chalk. 6⅜ x 4½ inches (163 x 115 mm.). Traces of red chalk along vertical crease. Watermark: Cartouche inscribed C L and Colle (similar to Heawood 3289).

This careful sketch of a female nude, chastely drawing a drapery around her body with both hands, is a preparatory drawing for one of the three daughters of William de Albanac or William de Albini (as his name appears in the *Dictionary of National Biography*) in the painting *William de Albanac Presenting His Three Daughters to Alfred III, King of Mercia*, which no longer exists. The father was shown presenting his daughters to Alfred III, King of Mercia, with the following words: "Here be my three daughters, chuse to wife which you list; but, rather than you should have one of them to your concubine, I would slay her with my own hand" (John Leland's *Itinerary*, VIII, 1710, p. 58). West's painting, which was executed for Charles Manners, fourth Duke of Rutland, a descendant of William de Albini, hung at Belvoir Castle, Leicestershire, where it was burned in the fire of 26 October 1816; it had been exhibited at the Royal Academy in 1778 (no. 331). The Rev. Irvin Eller (*The History of Belvoir Castle, from the Norman*

Conquest to the Nineteenth Century, London, 1841, p. 132) notes that a Mr. Rising assessed its value at 150 guineas. Its composition has survived in an engraving of 1782 by Jean-Baptiste Michel (1748–1804) which was published by John Boydell in London (Fig. 9). It is interesting to note that a print of West's painting was owned by George Washington and hung in the family dining room at Mount Vernon during his lifetime.

The Morgan drawing shows the body of the central figure in the group of the three daughters in the engraving; there, however, the head is seen in frontal view and the arrangement of the draperies differs somewhat. West used the head in profile for the daughter standing next to the father. It might be added that there is a drawing of the same subject by Füssli in the Winterthur Museum (Gert Schiff, *Johann Heinrich Füssli, 1741–1825*, Zürich, 1973, I, 2, p. 212).

20

Sketch for "The Death of the Earl of Chatham"
1970.11:54   PLATE 10

Black chalk on blue paper. 7⅜ x 11 inches (189 x 279 mm.). The personalities identified by the artist's inscriptions are: *Rockingham, Abingdon (?), Richmond, Camden, Shelbourne, Temple, Manchester, Portland, Mʳ Pitt, Cumberland, Secretarys of State (?), Mansfield, York,*

Canterbury, Chancellor, Brocklesby, Mahon. Verso: Black chalk sketch for the right half of the same composition. Watermark: None.

The drawing records the event which occurred in the House of Lords on 7 April 1778. The Duke of Richmond in an address to the King had urged the withdrawal of the British armed forces from the American colonies. After he had finished, the great statesman William Pitt, Earl of Chatham, who had been in ill health for some time, rose to answer him and to urge the extension of the war effort in America. Richmond replied, paying tribute to Chatham for his patriotism and recommending a peace treaty with America, whereupon Chatham on attempting to rise and speak, collapsed. He actually did not die on the spot but lived on for another month.

It appears that Benjamin West and John Singleton Copley—both Americans by birth—were, for a while, in competition to paint a commemorative picture of the above event. Horace Walpole recalled (*Book of Materials*, 1771, p. 113 [1785], Lewis-Walpole Library, Farmington, Conn.): "Mr. West made a small Sketch of the death of Lord Chatham, much better expressed & disposed than Copley's. It has none but the principal person's present; Copley's almost the whole peerage, of whom seldom so many are there at once, & in Copleys most are meer [sic] spectators, but the great merit of West is the principal Figure which has his crutch & gouty stockings, which express his feebleness & account for his death." It speaks for West's fairness of character that although he had started on this project with the King's approval, he generously relinquished it for the benefit of his fellow artist.

The Morgan sheet—recto and verso—apparently shows preliminary drawings for the sketch mentioned by Horace Walpole. The latter was most likely an oil sketch and may be identical with Lot 71 in George Robins' sale catalogue of 1829, p. 23, where its measurements are given as "2 feet 3 inches high by 2 feet 11 inches wide"; according to the notation in the copy of the sale catalogue at the Frick Art Reference Library, it was sold for forty-six guineas to a Mr. Morgan.

In the more important sketch on the recto of the drawing, the Peers of the Realm, among them Mr. Pitt, Jr., surround the stricken man who is attended by Dr. Richard Brocklesby and Viscount Mahon, Lord Chatham's son-in-law, represented kneeling beside him. The other members of the House of Lords form two groups at the right and left of the scene in the center. The Duke of Richmond, who has just spoken, is conspicuous in the foreground on the left. A few sketchy lines indicate the details of the room; one can discern some pilasters or columns, chandeliers, and the canopy of the throne at the upper right.

There is another more finished drawing of the central group in the Henry Huntington Library and Art Gallery, San Marino, California (Acc. No. 69.6; black, red, and white chalk on blue paper, 5¼ x 6½ inches). In this sketch, greater emphasis has been placed on the two principal figures, which have been moved into the foreground, while the members of the House of Lords—reduced in size and lined up closely—are relegated to a minor role.

The Morgan composition may be compared with that of West's earlier historical painting *The Death of General Wolfe*, dated 1770 (National Gallery of Canada, Ottawa), where the hero of the Battle of Quebec is depicted in a pose similar to that of the Earl of Chatham. There the composition is also divided into three groups; however, these groups are linked more closely in the drawing. Copley is known to have worked on the *Death of the Earl of Chatham* from 1779 to 1781 (cf. Jules D. Prown, *John Singleton Copley*, Cambridge, 1966, II, pp. 275–91) and since both artists at first competed for the commission, one may assume a date of about 1779 for the Morgan sheet.

21

Study for "The Crucifixion"

1970.11:17   PLATE 11

Black chalk on blue paper. 12⅜ x 9⅜ inches (314 x 238 mm.). Signed in black chalk at lower left: *B. West.* Watermark: None.

This drawing illustrates the last stage in Christ's martyrdom on the cross, specifically the ninth hour, as described in the Gospel of St. Matthew XXVII, 46–52: "And behold the veil of the temple was rent in twain from the top to the bottom; and the earth did quake, and the rocks rent; and the graves were opened; and many bodies of the saints which slept arose. . . ." A group of frightened men, among them two high priests recognizable by their mitres, have gathered in the foreground; behind them, the dead are seen emerging from their coffins and a column has been thrown from its base by the quake. In the background at the upper right is another group of terror-stricken people, one of them a woman wearing a headdress with flowing veil, which may characterize her as a pagan priestess. The upper left portion of the drawing has been left unfinished by the artist, only two lightly sketched crosses designate the place as Golgotha. The drawing may be a first idea for *The Crucifixion* intended for the King's Chapel, Windsor, one of the themes listed under the Gospel Dispensation in the *Supplement to La Belle Assemblée* (p. 14); it may, however, never have been executed on canvas. The drawing shows similarity in draughtsmanship with the sketch for the *Death of the Earl of Chatham* (see No. 20, which is also executed in black chalk on blue paper). A date of about 1780 may therefore be indicated for this drawing. A drawing for the heads of the two priests is at the Friends Historical Library, Swarthmore College (P.P. 285; black chalk on oatmeal paper, 7 x 7⅝ inches). There is another, more conventional version of *The Crucifixion* among the Library's group of West drawings (1970.11:56; see No. 104).

22

Birth of Eve
1970.11:48   PLATE 14

Pen and brown ink, brown wash, and body color. 2⅝ x 3⅝ inches (66 x 93 mm.). Border in gray wash on old mount. Laid down. Inscribed by the artist in graphite on the old mount: *Birth of Eve B. West.*

This small drawing, distinguished by its execution in pink and blue body color, shows Adam gazing adoringly at the appearance of the first woman, who emerges like a radiant vision from the encircling clouds. There is no mention of this rather unusual subject in any of the old catalogues of West's *oeuvre.* It may have been the design for one of those cabinet pictures which were so much in demand by the collectors of the period. The several vertical lines indicate that West tried to visualize various proportions for the composition. The medium as

well as the drawing style makes a date in the early 1780's seem likely.

Fig. 10   Studies for "The Ascension."
Swarthmore, Pennsylvania, Swarthmore College, Friends Historical Library.

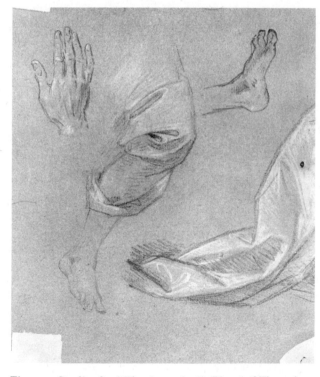

Fig. 11   Studies for "The Ascension" (Verso of Fig. 10).

23

Standing Male Figure and Other Sketches
Studies for *The Ascension*, the painting originally executed for the King's Chapel at Windsor, now at the War Memorial Chapel, Bob Jones University, Greenville, South Carolina.

1970.11:57　　　　　　　　　　　　PLATE 12

Black chalk, heightened with white, on blue paper faded to gray. 15⅛ x 14 inches (385 x 357 mm.). Horizontal crease in center, numerous stains throughout. Verso: Drapery study in the same medium. Watermark: None.

At some time in its history this drawing was cut into two parts, and it was in this condition that it entered the Library. When it was discovered that the small segment showing the bust of a male youth and hand exactly fitted into the right corner of the larger sheet, the two were reunited. This reunited sheet and the following drawing (Cat. No. 24) show preliminary studies for the figure of Christ and the two figures in the center of *The Ascension*. The studies of children's heads at the upper right of the first Morgan drawing may be portraits of two of the royal children; the head turned in three-quarter profile to the right is similar to Prince William's in West's *Portrait of the Princes William and Edward*, dated 1778, at Buckingham Palace. A further drawing at the Friends Historical Library, Swarthmore College (P.P. 222; F-1; same medium, 12⅝ x 10 inches), has on both recto and verso studies for the head of the apostle in the left foreground, the clasped hands of the figure behind him, as well as a number of details for the figure of the ascending Christ, that is, his face, hands, feet, and drapery (Figs. 10–11). There is an oil sketch on canvas of the entire composition at the Tate Gallery, London (49¾ x 28 inches. Fig. 12), and a finished drawing in black chalk, squared for transfer, was shown in the Benjamin West exhibition of 1968 at the Bernard Black Gallery in New York (*A Benjamin West Portfolio*, New York, 1968, no. 6, illus.). Two small compositional sketches in pencil are preserved at the Royal Library, Windsor Castle (17896 A, 140 x 75 mm.; 17896 B, 140 x 80 mm.).

Galt (*Life*, II, p. 213) lists the Bob Jones painting as *The Assumption of Our Saviour* under no. 34 in West's account book of the pictures he painted for the King from 1768 to 1780, as one of the pictures which was to decorate the King's new chapel at Windsor. The picture is also recorded in West's handwritten accounting for the paintings "he had the honour to make by His Majesty's commands for the Royal Palaces" from 1780 to 20 June 1797 (document at the Historical Society of Pennsylvania) under the year 1781 where he notes that he charged £1050 for it. From West's design for the decoration of one wall of the chapel (Fig. 13), which is now in the collection of Mr. and Mrs. Paul Mellon (it was formerly in the possession of Mrs. Claire Francis, one of the artist's descendants), we can see that *The Ascension* was to be the center piece in the decorative scheme of the wall,

Fig. 12　The Ascension. Oil Sketch.
London, Tate Gallery.

Fig. 13   Design for the Decoration of One Wall of the King's Chapel, Windsor Castle.
Collection of Mr. and Mrs. Paul Mellon, Upperville, Virginia.

which consisted of five large pictures with subjects from the New Testament and four smaller rectangular scenes from the Old Testament. *The Ascension* was exhibited at the Royal Academy, London, in 1782 as no. 144. It was included as Lot 169, page 59, in George Robins' catalogue of 22–52 May 1829, at which time most of the paintings remaining in West's house at No. 14 Newman Street, London, were sold at auction.

There are two other oil sketches by West representing *The Ascension*, one at the Washington County Museum of Fine Arts, Hagerstown, Maryland, signed and dated 1798, the other at the Newark Museum, Newark, New Jersey, but they evidently show a later and somewhat different version of the subject. These oil sketches are perhaps the preliminary studies for "a sketch for a large picture for His Majesty's chapel at Windsor, representing the Ascension of Our Saviour," which was exhibited at the Royal Academy, London, in 1801 (no. 167) and may be identical with the small *Ascension*, now in Lord Egremont's collection, Petworth House, Sussex, which, for the most part, was assembled by the third Earl of Egremont (1751–1837), the well-known patron of the fine arts.

24

Male Figure with Arms Outstretched and Two Details
Studies for the figure of Christ in *The Ascension*, Bob Jones University.

1970.11:122   PLATE 13

Black chalk, heightened with white, on blue paper. 14 x 12¼ inches (355 x 311 mm.). Vertical crease parallel to right margin; several stains. Verso: Three studies for a male portrait. Watermark: None.

See No. 23.

This study showing Christ's torso in the same attitude as in the painting is another example of West's careful preparation of the single figures in compositions of this period. Obviously he already had planned to cover the lower part of Christ's body with a drapery and so did not bother to represent it. In the painting he would change Christ's youthful face to a more mature type with beard and long hair.

The three studies for a male portrait on the verso of the Morgan drawing also demonstrate West's method of work (Fig. 14). The pose of the seated man slightly turned to the right as well as both hands emerging from elegantly ruffled sleeves are studied in great detail; the head, however, has not been drawn. It is hoped that one day the identity of the subject will be discovered.

25

Agrippina with Her Children Going through the Roman Camp

1970.11:211 PLATE 16

Black chalk. 4¾ x 7 inches (122 x 178 mm.). Verso: Landscape with hay wagon in black chalk. Watermark: None.

This small rough sketch may be a first idea for a composition representing yet another episode in the life of Agrippina as related in Tacitus' *Annals*, I–III (see No. 2). Galt (*Life*, II, p. 233) as well as the *Supplement to La Belle Assemblée*, p. 19, mentions "The sketch, in oil, (on paper) of the Procession of Agrippina with her Children and the Roman Ladies through the Roman Camp, when in Mutiny." There is a fine drawing of the subject at the Historical Society of Pennsylvania, Philadelphia (Vol. II of West drawings, p. 8; pen and brown ink on blue-gray paper, 12⁷⁄₁₆ x 9 inches. Fig. 15) which is authenticated by Benjamin West, Jr., on the back of the mount. The Library's drawing as well as the Philadelphia sheet shows Agrippina holding her son, the future emperor Gaius Caligula, on her arm, walking through the camp, and by her bravery persuading the mutinous soldiers serving under the command of Germanicus, her husband, to abandon their plans of revolt; some are seen bowing and kneeling in reverence to her and the Roman women accompanying her. The Philadelphia drawing, a vertical composition in contrast to the Morgan Library's horizontal rectangle, is executed with a very fine pen in West's drawing style of the 1780's; this may give an indication for dating the Morgan sketch.

26

The Resurrection
Compositional sketch for the central section

Fig. 14 Three Studies for a Male Portrait (Verso of Plate 24).

Fig. 15 Agrippina with Her Children Going Through the Roman Camp.
Philadelphia, Historical Society of Pennsylvania.

of the former choir window of St. George's Chapel, Windsor.

1970.11:44   PLATE 17

Black chalk on oatmeal paper. 12 ⅞ x 7½ inches (325 x 190 mm.). Watermark: None.

King George III took up residence at Windsor in about 1777. Between 1782 and 1792 a great deal of work was done at the King's expense in St. George's Chapel as is attested by the records, which are still preserved (*An Account of all the great works which have been executed in St. Georges Chapel Windsor . . . from the year 1782 to yᵉ end of 1792*. See William H. St. John Hope, *Windsor Castle, an Architectural History*, London, 1913, ii, Part 1, pp. 388–89). The plan to replace the gothic tracery and the old stained glass in the choir by a tripartite window of painted glass is mentioned as early as 1782. The King asked West to make the design, and Thomas Jarvis, a glass painter from Dublin, with his assistant Forrest, executed it. "The designs in colours on Canvas of our Saviours Resurrection and the Cartoons from those designs—thirty feet in height, by thirty feet in breadth . . ." are mentioned under the year 1782 in "Mr. Wests accompt for Paintings he had the honour to make by His Majesty commands for the Royal Palaces" (document in the Historical Society of Pennsylvania, Philadelphia). West charged the large sum of £2,200 for this work.

West's design, which was exhibited at the Royal Academy in 1783 as no. 16, showed the Resurrection in the center, the Three Marys approaching the sepulchre on the right, and Peter and John running toward the scene of the miracle on the left. It appears from the records that the window with West's design was actually put in place in 1786. In the course of the restoration of the east end of St. George's Chapel by G. G. Scott in 1863, West's transparency was removed and the window given its original gothic decoration, consisting, however, of modern stained glass. (A view of the choir showing the windows designed by West can be found in W. H. Pyne, *The History of the Royal Residences*, London, 1819, i, pl. opp. p. 182.)

West's design for the central portion of the east window in St. George's Chapel appears to have been preserved in the large painting of the Resurrection (118 x 52 inches. Fig. 16), now at the Museo de Arte, Ponce, Puerto Rico (cf. Julius S.

Fig. 16   The Resurrection.
Ponce, Puerto Rico, Museo de Arte.

Held, *Catalogue, I, Paintings of the European and American Schools*, Museo de Arte, Ponce, Puerto Rico, 1965, p. 194, pl. 159). The tall vertical format of the painting terminating in a gothic arch tends to support this assumption. On the basis of its measurements, which differ by only two inches on either side, the painting can perhaps be identified with *The Resurrection of Our Saviour* (120 x 54 inches), Lot 141 on page 42 of the George Robins sale catalogue of 1829; there it is described as "an awful, and most impressive composition, designed for the centre compartment of the Great Window." There is a drawing for the head of the Christ (pen and brown ink, 7 x 5¹³⁄₁₆ inches) at the Historical Society of Pennsylvania, Philadelphia (Vol. 1 of West Drawings, p. 4), which is inscribed on the back of the old mount by West's younger son, Benjamin: "Study for the head of Christ in the cartoon of the Resurrection, painted on glass by Jervis for St. George's Chapel – Windsor." There also is a squared pencil drawing of the entire composition in the Wilmington Society of Fine Arts, Wilmington, Delaware; it measures 23⅜ x 14¼ inches and is possibly a copy by the hand of an assistant, perhaps representing a stage in the working process.

The Morgan Library's compositional sketch is most likely a first idea for the design of the central portion of the east window for St. George's Chapel. The summary execution certainly speaks for this assumption. The "designs in colours on canvas" and the cartoons mentioned in West's account book and used for the painting on glass—one of the designs in colors on canvas may be the painting in Ponce—certainly go into greater detail. The sketch corresponds in all essential elements with the Ponce painting, except for the gesture of the angel who stretches out his arms toward Christ; even the man raising his right hand is noticeable in the foreground.

A preparatory drawing by West for the *Three Marys on Their Way to the Tomb* inscribed in a gothic arch, and signed and dated 1782, was formerly in the Robert Witt collection (see Iolo A. Williams, *Early English Watercolours*, London, 1952, pl. CIII, fig. 208). The painting of the subject is still preserved at Tatton Park (National Trust), Cheshire, England. It probably is identical with Lot 142 on page 43 of the George Robins sale catalogue of 1829 where its measurements are given as 5 feet 3 inches by 2 feet 10 inches. The original design for the left section of the window, *Peter and John Running towards the Sepulchre*, is mentioned as Lot 140, but the title is erroneously cited as "Peter and John Going from the Sepulchre." Its measurements are identical with those of the *Three Marys*. There is a preparatory drawing by West for *Peter*

and John Running towards the Sepulchre, also signed and dated *B. West 1783* and inscribed in a gothic arch, at the Boston Museum of Fine Arts (Acc. No. 42.616). *The Windsor Guide of 1798* published by C. Knight (pp. 63–65) gives a description of the remaining windows of the chapel: there was the Angel Appearing to the Shepherds in the east window of the south aisle, a Crucifixion in the large west window, and a Nativity and the Wise Men's Offering in the west windows of the south and north aisles.

27

The Risen Christ
Study for the central section of the former choir window of St. George's Chapel, Windsor.

1970.11:181   PLATE 18

Black chalk on oatmeal paper. 8¾ x 8⁹⁄₁₆ inches (223 x 218 mm.). Laid down. Watermark: None.

In the present study the *pentimenti* in the area of the face indicate that the artist first considered a profile view; otherwise, the figure is very close to that in the painting in Ponce.

See No. 26.

28

The Resurrection
1970.11:63

Black chalk. 6¼ x 4 inches (160 x 103 mm.). Irregular right margin. Watermark: Fragment.

This drawing on a sketchbook leaf may be another early compositional idea for the design of the large window in St. George's Chapel (see Cat. No. 26). The man in the center foreground, seen from the back raising his right hand, and the helmeted soldier holding a dagger in his right hand also appear in the painting at the Museo de Arte, Ponce, Puerto Rico.

29

Half-Length Figure Gazing Upward
1970.11:125

Brown and black chalk on blue paper. 7¾ x 6 ⁹⁄₁₆ inches (197 x 168 mm.). Watermark: None.

This figure of a man, with draped head, evidently awestruck by some event he is witnessing, may be compared with one of the men in the lower left corner of the painting of *The Resurrection*, now in Ponce, Puerto Rico (see No. 26). The facial type and the frightened gesture of the right hand are notably similar. If this study was not made in preparation for this painting, it may have been used for a similar miraculous scene.

30

Three Studies for the Figure of Christ in a "Resurrection"

1970.11:43   PLATE 19

Pen and brown ink. 11³⁄₁₆ x 6 inches (285 x 152 mm.). Laid down. Watermark: G R 1802.

This sheet of pen sketches affords an opportunity to study the artist's working method. In the sketch on the left, West represented Christ sitting on the edge of the sarcophagus, his head and arms raised toward heaven, his billowing shroud reinforcing the upward movement. Christ, on the right, is drawn in a quieter standing pose, the head in frontal view and the hands crossed over his chest. The third sketch in the upper half of the sheet shows Christ standing on clouds, his hands again crossed on his breast, the whole figure enclosed within a radiance. These sketches, too, are in subject and drawing style related to *The Resurrection* for St. George's Chapel, Windsor, and *The Ascension* for the King's Chapel, Windsor Castle (Christ in the sketch on the left raises his hands in a gesture similar to that of the Christ in the Bob Jones University painting, Nos. 23–24). It was not until the present catalogue was already well advanced that this drawing was removed from its old mount. It was then possible to decipher the watermark of 1802, thus placing this drawing somewhat later than had been previously surmised.

31

Christ and the Angel

1970.11:45   PLATE 20

Black chalk on gray paper; the head of Christ gone

Fig. 17   The Resurrection. Oil Sketch.
Philadelphia, Philadelphia Museum of Art, Given by Mr. and Mrs. D. Clifford Ruth.

over with pen and brown ink. 12¹¹⁄₁₆ x 8 inches (321 x 202 mm.). Soiled along upper and lower margin. Verso: Extensive application of black chalk. Watermark: Britannia (close to Heawood 235).

George Robins' sale catalogue of 1829 of Benjamin West's collection, in some of the descriptions of the individual pictures, stresses the fact that the connoisseurs of the period coveted those small cabinet pictures, and would have possessed them, had their author consented to part with them, at any price. The present drawing may have been made in preparation for just such a picture, possibly Lot 114 in this same catalogue entitled *Christ and the Angel* and described as "A chaste and most pleasing cabinet picture." The measurements, "2 feet high by 1 foot 6 inches," indicate that the painting was approximately twice the size of the drawing. There is a basic similarity between the Library's drawing and the oil sketch *The Resurrection* at the Philadelphia Museum of Art (67-195-1; oil on paper mounted on panel, 15¾ x 12 inches. Fig. 17); however, the title of the painting in the 1829 sale catalogue, "Christ and the Angel," seems more appropriate in connection with the drawing than with the oil sketch which, by the addition of a group of soldiers with shields and lances, has been enlarged to include all the participants in the scene of the Resurrection. The oil sketch like the Library's drawing shows Christ, both arms outstretched, emerging from the tomb, the entrance to which is outlined as a vertical rectangle. In the drawing the figure ascends the clouds while in the oil sketch he is shown walking down the steps from the tomb. The angel, his head turned toward Christ, sits on the stone of the sepulchre in the drawing. In the painting, however, the stone lies across the steps below the angel's feet. Perhaps the most significant difference between the drawing and painting is the addition of the group of soldiers at the lower right.

The type of Christ and the treatment of the body are comparable to that of Christ in the preparatory drawing for the Ponce *Resurrection* (1970. 11:181) and suggest a date in the 1780's for the Library's drawing and the Philadelphia oil sketch.

32

The Temptation of Christ
1970.11:180   PLATE 21

Black chalk on gray paper. 16⅜ x 11⅝ inches (416 x 294 mm.). Irregular left and lower margin; some foxing and creases at upper left corner; soiled along left margin. Watermark: Letter G.

This drawing may well be the sketch for *Christ's Temptation and Victory in the Wilderness* listed by Galt (*Life*, II, p. 212) as no. 25 in the series of religious paintings for the King's Chapel, Windsor Castle. Since Galt adds the words "a sketch" to the subject and does not cite the sum the artist was paid as he does for most of the paintings in this cycle, it may be assumed that the Temptation painting was never executed.

The drawing represents Christ standing on a mountaintop resisting the temptation of the Devil, who is seen departing in a rage at the lower right. Two angels are faintly indicated at the upper left. There is a *pentimento* in Christ's left arm; the artist at first intended to have Christ cross his hands on his chest. Similar in style to the study for the figure of Christ (1970.11:181) in the *Resurrection* for St.

George's Chapel, Windsor, this sheet, too, may have been executed in the early 1780's.

33

Esau Selling His Birthright for a Dish of Pottage
1970.11:66   PLATE 22

Brush and brown ink on light brown prepared paper. 7 x 10⅜ inches (178 x 264 mm.). Inscribed in graphite on recto, at upper left, *72*; at lower left, *£1:10*. Watermark: None.

This and the following two drawings (one of them a tracing) represent the well-known story from Genesis XXVII. Esau, characterized as the hunter with quiver and arrows, is seen sitting on his father's bed, gesturing toward an empty bowl. The blind Isaac propped up on a pillow feebly raises his hand and tells Esau: "Thy brother came with subtlety, and hath taken away thy blessing." Rebecca and Jacob who plotted together against Esau appear on the right, Rebecca evidently urging Jacob to go to her brother Laban for a while until his brother's anger subsides.

The early catalogues of West's works list only *The Birth of Jacob and Esau*, the painting originally intended for the King's Chapel at Windsor and exhibited at the Royal Academy in 1800 (no. 144); it is now at Bob Jones University, Greenville, South Carolina. However, the 1839 sale catalogue of West's drawings includes this item under no. 105: "Jacob and Esau. Outline, in reed pen and washed with sepia." Although the heavy lines of the brush could possibly be mistaken for the strokes of the reed pen, the complete absence of wash in the Library's drawing makes it unlikely that the catalogue refers to this sketch. *Esau Selling His Birthright* was perhaps one of the subjects which West composed for the King's Chapel, but which was never finally executed.

The composition recalls West's *King Lear and Cordelia*, the painting at the Henry E. Huntington Library and Art Gallery, which Robert R. Wark dates "probably in the 1780's" (*The Huntington Art Collection*, San Marino, California, 1970, p. 48, no. 66). The type of the ailing old king, the pose of Cordelia, the drapery as well as the two figures standing under the arch may be compared with those in the Library's drawing.

34

Esau Selling His Birthright for a Dish of Pottage

1970.11:157 PLATE 22

Black chalk. 2⅝ x 3⅞ inches (67 x 101 mm.). Watermark: C. Tay[lor].

This roughly sketched composition may be West's first idea of the subject. The disposition of the figures is the same as in the Library's brush drawing, only the gestures of the two protagonists are different. The classical ornament running along the lower edge of the bed in the preceding drawing can also be observed on the table in this sketch.

See No. 33.

35

Esau Selling His Birthright for a Dish of Pottage

1970.11:266

Pen and black ink on tracing paper. 8⅞ x 13⅛ inches (218 x 333 mm.). Vertical crease in center; irregular lower margin. Number 8.) appears at lower left. Watermark: None.

Despite the fact that this tracing is slightly larger than the drawing discussed in No. 33, it reproduces the main features of the composition. It is possibly the work of a studio hand.

See No. 33.

36

Joseph Making Himself Known to His Brothers

1970.11:207

Black chalk. 3⅝ x 3 ⁵⁄₁₆ inches (93 x 83 mm.). Small loss in upper right corner. Verso: Fragmentary sketch of a woman in red chalk. Watermark: None.

Galt (*Life*, II, p. 210) in his list of religious representations intended for the King's Chapel in Windsor Castle mentions as no. 6 in the category of Patriarchal Dispensation "Joseph and his Brothers in Egypt, composed, not painted." Were it not for its

small size, the Morgan drawing might be regarded as that referred to by Galt. It is an illustration of the well-known story from Genesis, Chapter XLIV. Joseph had commanded his steward to place one of his silver cups in Benjamin's sack; he then ordered his servant to stop and search his brothers on their way home from Egypt where they had come for food during a famine. On the discovery of the silver cup in Benjamin's sack, the boy was to be held by Joseph as a thief. In the Library's drawing, Judah, the eldest of Joseph's brothers, is seen kneeling before Joseph, who is seated at a round table, as he pleads with him to let Benjamin return with them to their old father, who would die of grief over the loss of his youngest son, especially since he believed that his other favorite son, Joseph, had long since been killed by a wild beast. The artist has chosen the moment when Joseph reveals his identity. The boy Benjamin, who is being held by Joseph's servant, and perhaps one of his brothers appear behind the two principal figures. A suspended curtain provides the backdrop for the scene which is illuminated by a classical oil lamp. The drawing probably dates from the time shortly after 1780 when the decoration of the King's Chapel was in the planning stage.

37

Oliver Cromwell Pointing to the Mace
Preliminary sketch for *Cromwell Dissolving the Long Parliament.*

1970.11:27 PLATE 23

Black chalk on blue paper. 6⅛ x 5⅜ inches (154 x 137 mm.). Laid down. Numbered 74 in graphite by a later hand in the lower left corner of the old mount. Watermark: None.

This is a preliminary sketch for the figure of Cromwell in West's historical painting *Cromwell Dissolving the Long Parliament*, now at the Montclair Art Museum, Montclair, New Jersey (Fig. 18). The painting is one of five historical scenes commissioned by the first Earl Grosvenor (1731–1802); the other four are *The Landing of Charles II at Dover*, now in a private collection in this country; *The Battle of the Boyne*, present location unknown; *The Battle of La Hogue*, now at the National Gallery of Art, Washington, D.C. (another version inscribed *B. West 1778, Retouched 1806* is at the Metropolitan Museum in New York); and *The Death of General Wolfe*, now at the National Gallery of Canada in Ottawa. These five pictures formerly hung in the library at Eaton Hall near Chester, England, the ancestral home of the Grosvenors. Two of them, the *Battle of La Hogue* and the *Landing of Charles II at Dover*, were sold at auction in 1959 (London, Sotheby & Co., The Property of the . . . Duke of Westminster, 15 July 1959, p. 29, nos. 125–26).

The painting *Cromwell Dissolving the Long Parliament* represents the event of 20 April 1653, when Cromwell, after having called in a band of musketeers, pointed first to the Speaker and then to the mace lying on the table with the words "Take away these baubles."

The Morgan drawing shows the full-length figure of Cromwell in essentially the same costume and pose as in the painting; however, his head is turned to the right instead of the left and he points to the mace with both hands whereas in the painting he holds a walking stick in his left hand. There is a compositional sketch for the picture at the Friends Historical Library, Swarthmore College (42; c-6. Fig. 19) showing the central group and the architectural setting. It is likewise executed in black chalk on blue paper and measures 9¾ x 11⅞ inches; Cromwell, bareheaded, is shown walking toward the table on which the mace has been placed. In the end West decided to portray Cromwell in a wide-brimmed hat similar to the one he is shown wearing in the Morgan drawing.

The painting is dated 1782 which provides a *terminus ante quem* for the Morgan drawing. The painting was exhibited at the Royal Academy in 1783 as no. 62 and John Hall (1739–17), engraver to His Majesty, made an engraving of the composition as well as of that of the *Battle of the Boyne* in 1781.

Fig. 18   Cromwell Dissolving the Long Parliament.
Montclair, New Jersey, Montclair Art Museum.

Fig. 19   Cromwell Dissolving the Long Parliament. *Swarthmore, Pennsylvania, Swarthmore College, Friends Historical Library.*

Fig. 20   Death on a Pale Horse. *London, Royal Academy.*

38

Head of a Cavalier

1970.11:75   PLATE 23

Black chalk, heightened with white, on blue paper.
4¾ x 3¹⁵⁄₁₆ inches (120 x 100 mm.). Laid down. The
number *73* in graphite by a later hand appears in the
lower left corner of the old mount. There are several
sketches in pen and gray ink by a different hand on the
back of the old mount. Watermark: None.

West may have made this sketch of a man in profile with long hair, moustache, pointed beard, and
white collar for a figure in the painting *Cromwell
Dissolving the Long Parliament*. The head, however,
does not appear in the painting.

39

Death on a Pale Horse (Revelation VI, 8)

1970.11:20   PLATE 24

Pen and brown ink over black chalk. 14 x 18¾ inches
(354 x 475 mm.). Verso: Torso of male nude seen
from the back, in black chalk. Watermark: Coat-of-
arms with fleur-de-lis surmounted by crown (close to
Churchill 415 and 416).

The Morgan drawing most likely represents a first
idea for one of Benjamin West's most famous and
important paintings. The subject was originally included in the picture cycle for the King's Chapel
at Windsor Castle as part of the Revelation Dispensation. The existence of a total of four compositional sketches including a drawing at the Royal
Academy, signed and dated *B West 1783 retouched
1803* (Fig. 20), three oil sketches, and the large
painting of 1817 at the Pennsylvania Academy of
Fine Arts, Philadelphia, is sufficient proof of the
artist's keen interest in the subject, which occupied
his imagination for more than three decades. The
first and third of the oil sketches dating from about
1787 and 1802 are at the Pennsylvania Museum of
Art; the second dated 1796 is in Lord Egremont's
collection at Petworth House, Sussex, England.
The composition was only slightly changed over
this long period, only the large painting of 1817
showing a major alteration in the rider on the
right who became Christ or the Messiah. It is a
prime example of West's "dread manner" and

epitomizes Edmund Burke's theories of the "ter-
rible sublime." It is interesting to note that West
took one of the small oil sketches with him to Paris
where it was shown in the exhibition of the same
year. Fiske Kimball, "Benjamin West au Salon de
1802," *Gazette des Beaux-Arts*, VII, 1932, pp. 403–10,
believed it was the version dated 1802; George
Robins' sale catalogue of 1829 which includes the
large painting now at the Pennsylvania Academy
of Fine Arts as Lot 98, however, states on page 31
that it was the Earl of Egremont's painting. With
its turbulent action and macabre theme, it may
have influenced the romantic inventions of Géri-
cault and Delacroix.

The Morgan drawing shows only part of the
composition. Death, depicted as a skeleton, is seen
riding over a mass of humanity in various attitudes
of terror. He wears a crown and clutches a bunch
of darts in each hand. A couple with a baby flees to
the right in the foreground. The same group appears in the Royal Academy drawing and in the
paintings where they are stretched out on the
ground, the woman frightened or already dead,
the man trying to fend off death with his raised
right arm. There are several wild beasts in the
Morgan drawing, one at the lower left and two at
the upper right. The latter, a lion and a wolf, can
be seen on the left in the other versions. The horse
on which Death is astride is not noticeably agitated
in the Morgan drawing; however, in the other
works it gradually assumes a wilder appearance in
the more violent turn of its head, the fierce look of
the eyes, and the open mouth, heightening the
dramatic impact of the scene. The intertwined
bodies of the two nudes in the horse's path on the
left in the drawing can also be found with some
variations in the Royal Academy drawing as well
as in the painted versions. One may perhaps conclude on the basis of these observations that the
Morgan drawing, which lacks many vital elements of the composition—the group of three
horsemen on the right, the crouching old man, and
the demons behind the figure of Death—is an
early sketch preceding the drawing at the Royal
Academy.

Norman Ziff has recently pointed out that the
etching *Death on a Pale Horse* by Joseph Haynes
after a drawing by John Hamilton Mortimer
(1740–79), which was published on 1 January
1784, may have been a source of inspiration for

Benjamin West. See Norman D. Ziff, "Mortimer's 'Death on a Pale Horse'," *Burlington Magazine*, CXII, 1970, pp. 531–35.

The drawing *Death on a Pale Horse* at the Wilmington Society of the Fine Arts, Wilmington, Delaware, although bearing the initials *B.W.*, may well be a studio work while the drawing no. 14 in the catalogue of the West exhibition of 1968 at the Bernard Black Gallery in New York with its overdramatization and nervous broken pen lines is possibly by the hand of West's son Raphael.

40

Seated Figure of Christ
Study for *The Last Supper*, Tate Gallery, London.

1970.11:179   PLATE 26

Black chalk. 4¼ x 5⁵⁄₁₆ inches (108 x 135 mm.). Watermark: None.

The figure of Christ reclining at the table in Roman fashion appears unchanged in the Tate painting (Fig. 21). There, too, he holds a piece of bread in his left hand and gestures toward the chalice with his right hand.

Galt (*Life*, II, p. 212), in Appendix No. 1 which contains a list of the "Pictures painted by Benjamin West for His Majesty . . . from 1768 to 1780," mentions as entries 28 and 29 two pictures of the Last Supper, one for St. George's Chapel, Windsor, the other for the King's Chapel; West charged the same amount for both pictures, namely £735.

Fig. 21   The Last Supper.
London, Tate Gallery.

One can perhaps conclude on the basis of this information that West worked on two paintings of the subject simultaneously and that the Tate Gallery painting is possibly the altarpiece intended for the King's Chapel. The records of the Royal Academy exhibitions, which include a design for a Last Supper for His Majesty's chapel in Windsor Castle in 1784 (no. 437) and a painting of this subject for the same chapel in 1785 (no. 219), support this assumption.

In West's watercolor sketch for the east side of the King's Chapel, which is preserved at the Royal Library, Windsor Castle (17863; 310 x 284 mm.), he shows a painting of the Last Supper over the communion table. In this composition, which may be a first idea for the altarpiece, Christ and the apostles are seated around a table against the background of an arch opening into a landscape, a setting also effectively used in the compositional sketch for St. George's Chapel discussed in the following entry. Conforming to a neo-classical concept, West changed the background in the Tate Gallery painting to a wall niche in the form of an arch, retaining, however, the drapery, the oil lamp, and the column at right.

41

The Last Supper
Compositional sketch for the altar painting in St. George's Chapel, Windsor.

1970.11:214   PLATE 27

Black chalk. 5¹³⁄₁₆ x 8½ inches (148 x 217 mm.). Small tear at center of left margin; diagonal crease at upper right corner. Verso: Black chalk sketch of Venus and Cupid, and a seated male nude in a landscape. Watermark: None.

Soon after George III had requested West to make the design for the Resurrection window in St. George's Chapel, he commissioned him to paint a large picture of the Last Supper to be placed over the communion table. West's account book at the Historical Society of Pennsylvania entitled "Pictures and Cartoons painted by commands of His Majesty by Benjⁿ West" mentions under the year 1786 "The picture of the Last Supper which His Majesty made a present of to the Collegiate Church

Windsor"; its cost is marked as £735. It should be noted, however, that the original sketch for the *Last Supper* over the communion table in the Collegiate Church, Windsor, was not exhibited at the Royal Academy until 1804. The painting is still in existence today (cf. Helmut von Erffa, "Benjamin West at the Height of His Career," *The American Art Journal*, I, no. 1, 1969, p. 29).

The composition of the freely sketched Morgan sheet is very similar to that of the painting. The most striking difference is in the figure of Judas who looms large in the foreground of the painting and, by his size, draws attention away from the Christ, the spiritual focus of the event. As a matter of fact, some of the critics of the period objected to the predominance of the figure of Judas although others praised the picture as a masterly composition. Judas, in the drawing, is not as prominent as in the painting; a figure of average height, he is seen leaving the room at the extreme right. John Thomas Smith notes in his book of recollections, *A Book for a Rainy Day* (London, 1845, p. 77), that he had sat for the head of St. John in West's picture of the *Last Supper* for the altar of St. George's Chapel, Windsor.

A study for the altarpiece for St. George's Chapel, Windsor, 10½ inches high by 14 inches wide, was included in George Robins' sale catalogue of 1829 as Lot 21.

42

Head of Caparisoned Horse
Preparatory sketch for the painting *Edward the Third Crossing the Somme*, now at Kensington Palace, London.

1970.11:194   PLATE 25

Black chalk, heightened with white, on gray paper. 5⅞ x 8⅞ inches (149 x 226 mm.). Verso: Black chalk sketch of ornamented bridle strap (?). Watermark: None.

The painting, which West executed for the King's Audience Chamber at Windsor Castle, is signed and dated *B. West. 1788* (see Oliver Millar, *The Later Georgian Pictures in the Collection of Her Majesty the Queen*, London, 1969, no. 1158, pl. 125). It was exhibited at the Royal Academy in 1792 (no. 66). A small oil sketch, also signed and dated *B. West 1788*, was recently on the New York art market.

43

Edward the Third and the Black Prince
Preparatory sketch for the painting *Edward III with the Black Prince after the Battle of Crécy*, now at St. James's Palace, London.

1970.11:217

Pen and brown ink. 3½ x 5⅜ inches (89 x 137 mm.). Watermark: None.

This small pen sketch shows the two principal figures of the painting in reversed position (see Oliver Millar, *op. cit.*, nos. 1164–66, pl. 126). The painting is signed and dated *B. West 1789* and, as Millar suggests, may be a small replica of the large picture also painted by West for the King's Audience Chamber, since 1968 on loan in the Palace of Westminster. The Black Prince in the Morgan drawing wears a plumed helmet while he appears bareheaded in the painting; Edward III's helmet is more elaborate in the painting than in the drawing. There is a signed compositional sketch at the Philadelphia Museum of Art (39.15-3; pen, ink, and wash, 9½ x 18¼ inches).

44

Costume Studies
1970.11:210   PLATE 28

Pen and brown ink on oatmeal paper. 4¹³⁄₁₆ x 7 inches (122 x 178 mm.). Stains at upper and lower center. Color notations in pen and brown ink: *Black* | $\frac{Black}{Gold}$ | $\frac{Gold}{White}$. Verso: Landscape in black chalk. Watermark: None.

The bearded man in the long robe and high hat in the lower part of the sheet may be significantly compared with one of the principal figures in the *Burghers of Calais*, the painting signed and dated *B. West. 1789*, now at Kensington Palace, London (see Oliver Millar, *op. cit.*, no. 1161, pl. 128). Dr. Roy Strong of the Victoria & Albert Museum, in one of his lectures in the Franklin Jasper Wall series at the Morgan Library, pointed out the influence of Joseph Strutt's publication *A Complete View of the Dress and Habits of the People of England*, London, 1796–99, on historical painting in England and, following this lead, it was discovered that the three figures in the lower half of the Mor-

Fig. 22   Christ Blessing Little Children.
London, Foundling Hospital (Thomas Coram Foundation for Children).

gan sheet can be found on plates LXX, LXXVII, and LXXVIII of Volume II of Strutt's work where they are listed as copies from a fourteenth-century manuscript *Chroniques de France ou de Saint Denis* in the Royal Library at the British Museum (20 C VII). Since West's painting the *Burghers of Calais*, in which the bearded, robed figure with the high headdress appears in modified form, is dated 1789 —ten years before the publication of the second volume of Strutt's book—and since the couples in the upper half of the Morgan sheet do not seem to be included in Strutt's publication, one may assume that West had access to the manuscript itself in the King's Library. This seems to be confirmed by the fact that two figures in the Morgan drawing, the man with the high headdress and the courtier next to him, appear on one and the same page in the manuscript (folio 216) and that the headdress of the former shows a peak as in the manuscript but no such detail is to be found in Strutt's illustration on plate LXXVIII.

The freely sketched landscape on the verso shows a charming rural setting with a small bridge in the middleground; the *Landscape with Trees and*

Haywagon on the verso of *Agrippina with Her Children Going Through the Roman Camp* (No. 25), which is identical in size, may come from the same sketchbook.

45

Medieval Knight on Horseback
1970.11:262

Black chalk, heightened with white, on heavy brown paper. 10⅝ x 6⅜ inches (269 x 163 mm.). Verso: Two studies of birds in black chalk. Watermark: None.

This summary sketch of a knight in armor on horseback, although not identifiable with any particular painting, may well have been drawn in connection with West's series of paintings illustrating the history of Edward III for the King's Audience Chamber at Windsor Castle.

46

Christ Blessing Little Children
1970.11:219

Black chalk, heightened with white, on blue paper. 7⅛ x 11⅜ inches (180 x 288 mm.). Loss at lower left corner. Verso: Sketch for *Christ among the Doctors* (?). Watermark: None.

The drawings on either side of the Morgan sheet can perhaps be related to the paintings executed by West for the Duke of Rutland and mentioned in the *Supplement to La Belle Assemblée of 1808* on page 19: "Christ among the Doctors – Its companion, Christ blessing little Children; both painted for the late Duke of Rutland, and at Belvoir Castle." Unfortunately, these paintings were destroyed in the fire of 26 October 1816. The Rev. Irvin Eller (*The History of Belvoir Castle, from the Norman Conquest to the Nineteenth Century*, London, 1841, p. 204) quotes the value of the two "small" pictures lost in the fire, as assessed by a Mr. Rising, as £40 each (he erroneously cites the title of one of the pictures as "Samuel Presented to Eli").

A comparison of the Library's drawing *Christ Blessing Little Children* with the painting of the same subject still preserved at the Foundling Hospital, London (oil on canvas, 85 x 73½ inches. Fig. 22), shows a similar, though reversed arrangement of the figures in front of a column and an arch opening into a landscape. However, the horizontal composition has been changed to a vertical format, and the kneeling woman holding a child in the right foreground appears in frontal view to the left of Christ in the painting. According to information kindly furnished by Mr. Swinley, Director and Secretary of the Thomas Coram Foundation for Children, London, West originally executed the painting for Macklin's Bible (published in London in 1800); it was presented by four of the Governors to the Foundling Hospital in 1801.

The engraving after the painting made by John Hall is dated 1795. The "finished sketch" was exhibited at the Royal Academy in 1792 (no. 421); it may be identical with a small painting of the subject (oil on canvas, 22 x 16 inches), signed and dated 1791, in a private collection. West painted another picture of the subject in 1810 which was included in a Royal Academy exhibition of that year (no. 92); a preparatory outline drawing in pen and brown ink (7¹¹⁄₁₆ x 6⅛ inches), signed and dated *B. West 1810*, at the Historical Society of Pennsylvania, Philadelphia (Vol. 1 of West drawings, p. 2), shows a composition reduced to only three figures, including the kneeling woman who appears on the right of the Morgan sketch. As the latter is closer in composition and drawing style to the Foundling Hospital painting, a date in the 1790's is suggested here. There is another painted version of the subject at the Royal Academy, London (oil on canvas, 44½ x 83¼ inches); like the Morgan drawing, it is a horizontal composition, but otherwise differs considerably.

The sketch on the verso of the Morgan drawing, if it represents *Christ Conversing with the Doctors*, would be the companion to the composition on the recto, a plausible assumption in view of the similarity of the setting, a column and an open arch forming the background.

47

Design for a Medal
1970.11:156

Black chalk. 4 x 3⅝ inches (100 x 91 mm.). Verso: Fragment of sketch in black chalk. Watermark: None.

This small design for a medal shows Britannia, a lion at her feet, flanked by two female figures both holding shields. The date 1790 appears on the base on which they are standing. The artist drew the figure of Britannia separately in profile at the lower right; she wears a plumed helmet and carries trident and shield.

Farington notes in his diary on 30 December 1793 (I, p. 31) that on this day West showed him "a design he had made for the commemorative medal" (i.e., a medal commemorating the twenty-fifth anniversary of the Royal Academy). His description of the medal corresponds with West's design at the Ashmolean Museum, Oxford, which is signed and dated *B. West 1793* and shows the bust of George III on the obverse and three female figures representing Architecture, Painting, and Sculpture on the reverse. Farington on 14 April 1794 (I, p. 46) reports that West had to give up the competition for the design of the medal because, as his colleague, the painter Northcote put it, "He ought not to grasp at or expect every honor, that the Academy had clothed him with a robe of velvet, but that He should not struggle for every stripe of ermine." According to information received from Mr. Philip James, Librarian of the Royal Academy, the medal, an example of which exists in the British Museum, was actually designed by Robert Smirke in 1795 and the dies were executed by the medalist Lewis Pingo (1743–1830).

Although the diameter of the Morgan Library's design is identical with that in the Ashmolean's sketch and although both drawings show a group of three women, the different allegorical representation as well as the date (1790) makes the association of the Morgan sketch with the Royal Academy's anniversary medal rather tenuous. West may have made the Morgan Library's sketch with another occasion in mind.

48

Noah's Sacrifice
1970.11:161

Black chalk. 3¼ x 3¹⁄₁₆ inches (90 x 77 mm.). Verso: Printed invitation for dinner at the Free-Masons Tavern, Queen Street, dated January 179[?]. Watermark: None.

This and the following drawing are preparatory sketches for one of the paintings intended for the

King's Chapel at Windsor. Another drawing, formerly on the New York art market (pen and wash, 4¼ x 8½ inches), shows a horizontally extended composition in which several figures holding sacrificial animals have been introduced. That the large painting was actually completed is confirmed by its listing in West's account book appended to Galt's *Life* as no. 3; the amount West charged the King is posted as £525. The painting also was included in George Robins' sale catalogue as Lot 53 on page 18. Its measurements, 11 feet 6 inches high by 6 feet wide, would indicate that it was executed in a vertical format. Its fate is unknown. The scene in the present drawing shows Noah and his family sacrificing and giving thanks for their preservation during the Flood. Noah is seen in profile standing next to the altar and stretching out his arms in the manner of an orant. The dinner party invitation on the verso provides a date in the 1790's for this and the following drawing.

49

Noah's Sacrifice
1970.11:252

Pen and brown ink. 3⅞ x 3⅛ inches (98 x 78 mm.). Arched top. Watermark: None.

Noah is seen from the back raising his arms in an adoring gesture as smoke rises from the altar in front of him. The rounded top may indicate that the final painting was to be fitted into an arch at the King's Chapel.

50

The Expulsion of Adam and Eve
1970.11:65   PLATE 29

Black chalk. 7⅝ x 4⅞ inches (194 x 124 mm.). Watermark: None.

This rather moving sketch of Adam and Eve may be a first idea for the painting *Expulsion from Paradise* intended for the King's Chapel, Windsor. According to West's account book at the Historical Society of Pennsylvania, Philadelphia, the painting was completed in 1791 and the amount West charged the King is listed as £525. It was exhibited

at the Royal Academy in the same year (no. 147) and is identical with Lot 154 of George Robins' 1829 sale catalogue where its measurements are given as 6 feet high by 9 feet wide.

The artist very skillfully combined the two figures in one closely knit group. Eve, her long hair covering her nude body, seems to be weeping while Adam, his arms about her waist, tries to console her. There are *pentimenti* in the area of Adam's head. The undulating, often parallel lines add to the harmonious effect of the drawing.

51

Moses Destroying Pharaoh and His Host in the Red Sea
Study for the painting, now lost, originally executed for the King's Chapel, Windsor Castle.

1970.11:21   PLATE 30

Pen and brown ink over preliminary indications in black chalk on oatmeal paper. 14⅛ x 12¼ inches (360 x 311 mm.). Several creases along left margin; soiled areas along left and right margins. Watermark: None.

The Morgan drawing may be a first idea for the upper part of the composition which has survived in an oil sketch, now at the Worcester Art Museum, Worcester, Massachusetts (Acc. No. 1960.18; see Helmut von Erffa, "A Lost Painting by Benjamin West," *Worcester Art Museum News Bulletin*, XXVI, no. 4, January 1961). As Prof. von Erffa pointed out, this oil sketch is listed in George Robins' sale catalogue as Lot 168 and the large finished version as Lot 150. Galt (II, p. 210) mentions this painting as no. 10 under the heading "The Mosaical Dispensation."

A compositional drawing of the subject in the Boston Museum of Fine Arts (Acc. No. 42.602; pen and wash, 12¾ x 9⅞ inches. Fig. 23) varies considerably from that of the oil sketch. The Morgan sheet is closer to the Boston drawing than to the Worcester Museum's oil sketch; it seems to represent a stage preceding the Boston composition. Both drawings show Moses, with outstretched arms, a staff in his right hand, standing on a rocky ledge, the two nude men carrying the ark of the covenant, as well as the angel amid the billowing clouds. The figure of Aaron, however, is seen look-

Fig. 23 Moses Destroying Pharaoh and His Host in the Red Sea.
Museum of Fine Arts, Boston, Gift in Memory of John H. Sturgis by His Daughters.

ing up at Moses at the lower right in the Morgan drawing, while he appears behind Moses in the Boston sheet and the Worcester oil sketch.

The Destruction of Pharaoh and His Host is mentioned in West's account book at the Historical Society of Pennsylvania, under the year 1792; in the same year *The Triumph of Moses over Pharaoh and His Host* was exhibited at the Royal Academy (no. 124). A date of about 1792 may, therefore, be assumed for both the drawings and the Worcester oil sketch.

The figure of Moses is similar to that in the drawings for *Moses and the Brazen Serpent* at the Addison Gallery of American Art, Andover, Massachusetts, one of which is signed and dated 1790.

52

Aaron Staying the Plague
1970.11:235   PLATE 31

Pen and brown ink. 4$\frac{15}{16}$ x 4$\frac{15}{16}$ inches (126 x 126 mm.).

Signed in black chalk at lower right: *B. West*. Watermark: None.

This spirited drawing can be related to the sketch, presumably in oil, *Aaron Stopping the Plague*, which was exhibited at the Royal Academy in 1792 (no. 319), and to the line engraving by Henry Moses published in 1811 in *The Gallery of Pictures Painted by Benjamin West Esq.ʳ*, pl. v. (The Morgan Library's copy of this book bears the inscription: *Mrs. Thomas G. Margary / with Dr. Forbes Winslow's kind regards / April 1860*; it was given to Benjamin West's granddaughter, Maria.) The engraving, in turn, may reproduce the oil sketch which was included in George Robins' 1829 sale catalogue of West paintings (Lot 149 on p. 45), although the measurements, 2 feet 4 inches high by 3 feet 1 inch wide, indicate that this was a horizontal composition. West often extended his compositions horizontally by the addition of several figures.

The Morgan drawing and the Moses engraving illustrate the passage in Numbers XLVII–XLVIII: Aaron is seen standing between the dead and the living, swinging the censer, a gesture of atonement to stay the plague inflicted as punishment on the people of Israel for the rebellion of Korah, Dathan, and Abiram. Aaron's pose has been somewhat changed in the engraving, although the movement of his arms remains the same. The stricken people and those still untouched by the plague are concentrated in the lower part of the composition in the print, thus giving dominance to the main figure; in the drawing, however, the crowd surges turbulently around Aaron, with a face visible here and there.

53

Three Sketches of Venus Rising from the Sea
1970.11:203

Black chalk. 9$\frac{11}{16}$ x 5$\frac{13}{16}$ inches (245 x 147 mm.). Irregular right and left margins. Watermark: None.

These charming sketches relate to one of West's compositions preserved in an outline engraving by Moses as plate II in his *Gallery of Pictures Painted by Benjamin West Esq.ʳ*, the series of sixteen engravings published in 1811 and dedicated to the art patron Thomas Hope. George Robins' 1829 sale cata-

[33]

logue includes a painting of the same subject, referred to as *Venus Attired by the Graces* (p. 25, Lot 78), which is almost identical in size with the painting *Venus Borne by Swans with Cupid and Attired by the Graces*, listed in Christie's sale catalogue of 18 December 1959 as no. 100; the latter, coming from the collection of John Allnut, 1863, is signed and dated 1793 and was retouched in 1806. The three small sketches of the Morgan sheet show the group of Venus and Cupid in varying poses and relationships. In the sketch on the right, Venus is rather similar to the figure in the engraving; Cupid, however, is placed on the right. In the print the figures of the Three Graces have been added at the upper right.

The author of the commentaries (signed R.H.) which accompany Moses' engravings mentions the Venus de Medici as the inspiration for West's goddess of love and beauty, and there is a certain affinity in the chaste gesture of the left hand and the stance of the figure on the Morgan sheet and the Moses print with the Hellenistic statue.

The sketchbook leaf 1970.11:208 (No. 182) includes a small figure of Cupid with his bow which may possibly have been a preliminary sketch for the figure stringing his bow to the left of Venus in Moses' engraving after West's painting *Venus Rising from the Sea* (Moses, *op. cit.*, pl. II).

54

Christ
Study for the figure in *The Baptism*, the painting originally executed for the King's Chapel at Windsor, now at the War Memorial Chapel, Bob Jones University, Greenville, South Carolina

1970.11:16   PLATE 32

Black chalk, heightened with white, on gray paper. 15 x 9⅝ inches (380 x 243 mm.). Watermark: None.

The Baptism of Christ, which is listed as no. 24 in West's account book appended to Galt's *Life* (II, p. 212) and for which he charged the King the sum of £1,050, was exhibited at the Royal Academy in 1794 as *The Holy Spirit Descending upon Christ after His Baptism at the River Jordan* (no. 132). The decorative scheme for the north side of the King's Cha-

pel—as it appears in the Mellon collection's sketch (Fig. 13)—shows *The Baptism* to the left of *The Ascension*, which forms the centerpiece, and next to *Christ Healing the Sick in the Temple*. The large painting of *The Baptism* was included in George Robins' sale catalogue of 1829 as Lot 72 (the measurements, 12 feet 6 inches high by 10 feet wide, differ only slightly from those given in the Bob Jones 1963 catalogue *Revealed Religion*, namely 148 x 115 inches). George Robins' 1829 catalogue further mentions a smaller version of the subject, Lot 130 on page 40, which may be identical with no. 79 in Sotheby's sale catalogue of 19 July 1972 (measurements, 36 x 28 inches; bought by the Herner Wengraf Gallery, London, for £900). The 1839 sale catalogue of West drawings mentions "The Baptism of Our Saviour. Outline, in bistre and washed with the same," but this drawing remains unlocated to date. A somewhat different, possibly later version of the composition appears in the Stanford Museum's sketch (pencil, pen, and colored chalk, 156 x 297 mm.) and in the Detroit study of 1813

Fig. 24   Christ from "The Baptism." Lithograph. *New York, The New York Public Library, Astor, Lenox and Tilden Foundations, Prints Division.*

(Acc. No. 48.212; ink and wash, 5¾ x 9 inches) where the scheme has been expanded into a horizontal format by the addition of a large group of people on the right.

Christ in this fine Morgan drawing as well as in the Bob Jones painting is seen walking away from the river onto the bank. He faces toward the right, his slightly bowed head in strict profile and his hands crossed over his breast; part of his cloak is draped over his arm and falls to the ground between his feet. The figure of Christ served as the model for West's lithograph, signed and dated 1802, which is in the reverse direction and bears the inscription *This is my beloved son xc.* Impressions may be seen in the Joseph Pennell collection, New York Public Library (Fig. 24), and the Metropolitan Museum. There is an outline drawing of the figure of Christ at the Friends Historical Library, Swarthmore College (BWS 41; black chalk, 10⁹⁄₁₆ x 8⅞ inches, verso covered with black chalk for the purpose of tracing). Since it corresponds in every detail with the print, except that the figure faces right as in the Morgan study, it may be the drawing which West transferred to the lithographic stone.

Lithography, the graphic technique invented by Alois Senefelder in 1796, became popular in England as early as 1801 under the name of "Polyautography." Many famous artists, West, Stothard, Barry and Fuseli among them, contributed to the album *Specimens of Polyautography* published by Philip André in 1803. West's lithograph *The Angel at the Tomb* of 1801 and Raphael West's *Study of a Tree* of 1802 were included in this album.

Bibliography: *Sixteenth Report to the Fellows of the Pierpont Morgan Library, 1969–1971*, p. 107, pl. 23.

55

Moses Consecrating Aaron and His Sons to the Priesthood
1970.11:250

Pen and brown ink. 7¹⁄₁₆ x 4¾ inches (180 x 120 mm.). Verso: Figure of priest with knife; also fragment of compositional sketch. Watermark: Vryheyt (similar to Churchill 107, p. LXXV).

A painting of this subject is listed in West's "accompt / for Paintings he had the / honour to make by His / Majesty commands for the Royal Palaces"; the date of completion is recorded as 1795 and its cost as £1,050. The painting was intended for the King's Chapel, Windsor Castle (see Galt, *Life*, II, p. 210), and was exhibited at the Royal Academy in 1795 (no. 144). It may be identical with *Moses and Aaron Sacrificing*, Lot 51, page 18, in George Robins' 1829 sale catalogue; a smaller version of *Moses Consecrating Aaron and His Sons* is mentioned on page 40 (Lot 133) of the same catalogue. According to a notation in the margin of the Frick Library's copy, the smaller painting was purchased by the enamel painter Henry Bone (1755–1834) for 100 guineas. The fate of the two paintings is not known at present.

The Morgan sketch, in accordance with the Old Testament passage in Exodus XXIX, shows Moses in the center; Aaron in the costume of a high priest, knife in hand, stands ready to sacrifice the bull on the altar at right while Aaron's two sons watch the proceedings. The figure on the verso is a study of Aaron in full regalia, holding a knife and wearing the mitre-like headdress and the breastplate of the high priest.

56

Harvesters near Windsor Castle
1970.11:201   PLATES 34 AND 35

Black chalk. 7⁷⁄₁₆ x 6 inches (188 x 158 mm.). Loss at right margin; seal at left center has been pasted over. Inscribed in pen and brown ink: – *West Esqʳ.* Verso: Three sketches of landscape and a reaper in black chalk. Inscribed in pen and brown ink: . . . *Dʳ. Löchnern* . . . *Majesty.* Watermark: Fragment of coat-of-arms (close to Heawood 446).

West executed several paintings illustrating scenes from James Thomson's poem *The Seasons.* One of them, *The Washing of Sheep*, signed and dated 1795, is now at the Fine Arts Collection, Rutgers University, New Brunswick, New Jersey (see H. von Erffa, "West's 'The Washing of Sheep,' Genre or Poetic Portrait?," *The Art Quarterly*, XV, 1952, pp. 160–65, fig. 1); another, *Harvest Home*, which was exhibited at the Royal Academy in 1795, is now in a private collection (see H. von Erffa, "Benjamin West Reinterpreted," *Antiques*, LXXXI, June 1962, pp. 630–33, fig. 6). Both recto and verso of the Morgan sheet may show some preliminary ideas for the painting, which was included in George Robins' 1829 sale catalogue as Lot 64, page 21, *Reapers, with a View near Windsor* (19½ inches high x 27 inches wide). When drawing the figures of the reapers, West may well have had in mind the following lines of the poem:

> "Before the ripened field the reapers stand,
>   in fair array; . . .
> At once they stoop and swell the
>   lusty sheaves. . . ."

The summary outlines of the buildings in the background seem to suggest the familiar silhouette of Windsor Castle.

57

Rustic Lovers Struck by Lightning
1970.11:52   PLATE 33

Black chalk on light brown paper. 7⁷⁄₁₆ x 9 inches (189 x 299 mm.). Some foxing. Watermark: None.

Like the previous drawing, this may be an illustration of James Thomson's epic poem *The Seasons*. In the part devoted to "Summer," there is a story of two young lovers, Celadon and Amelia, who are caught in a thunderstorm, oblivious in their bliss of any danger until the girl is struck down by a flash of lightning. The 1839 sale catalogue of West drawings includes under nos. 112 and 112* a pair of drawings representing *Rustic Lovers Forewarned of the Approach of a Thunder Storm* and its companion, *Rustic Lovers Struck by Lightning*, executed in "bistre and colours, heightened with white." Although the latter title seems to imply that both lovers were killed by lightning, the compiler of the catalogue may have given an inaccurate description. The Morgan drawing gives vivid illustration to the poet's lines: "that moment, to the ground, A blackened corse, was struck the beauteous maid. But who can paint the lover, as he stood, Pierc'd by severe amazement, hating life, Speechless, and fix'd in all the death of woe! . . ."

58

The Toilet of Venus
1970.11:236   PLATE 36

Black chalk. 7⅛ x 6 inches (181 x 153 mm.). Signed in

black chalk at lower right: *B. West*. Label on mat bears number *322*. Watermark: None.

Among the Italian artists whom West most admired and whose works he collected were Raphael and Titian. At the time of his death, he owned Titian's *Death of Actaeon*, now at the National Gallery, London; a study for *Diana and Callisto*, the picture in the Duke of Sutherland's collection, at the National Gallery of Scotland; and a sketch for *The Last Supper* at the Escorial. In 1809 he offered Titian's *Venus and Adonis* to Richard H. Davis for £2,000. Titian certainly was the inspiration for West in this appealing Morgan drawing. The composition recalls Titian's *Lady at Her Toilet* in the Louvre where the young woman holds a strand of hair which falls over her shoulder in a similar fashion. Cupid, too, holding a rectangular mirror, may have been lifted by West from another of Titian's paintings such as *The Toilet of Venus* at Leningrad, which he might have known from a print. In addition, the motif of the garment draped over one shoulder and exposing one breast possibly has its precedent in the figure of Diana in *The Death of Actaeon. The Bacchante*, signed and dated *B. West 1797* in the Philip I. Berman collection, Allentown, Pennsylvania, was likewise clearly inspired by Titian's portrait of his daughter Lavinia, now in Berlin (Allentown, Pennsylvania, Allentown Art Museum, "The World of Benjamin West," 1962, p. 59, no. 23, illus.). The Library's drawing may perhaps date from this same period when the Venetian master exerted such a strong influence on West. It is a particularly good example of West's eclecticism.

59

The Angel in the Sun (Revelation XIX, 17)
1970.11:24   PLATE 38

Graphite. 9¼ x 9⅜ inches (237 x 239 mm.). Nearly a quarter of the sheet is missing at the lower right. Fragmentary inscriptions in pen and brown ink: on recto, *. . . kind respects to | West, & is much obliged*; on verso, *Mrs. West | Newman street*. Watermark: IV 1794.

On the left side of the vertical line dividing the drawing is the Angel in the Sun standing on a rocky ledge in front of a circular radiance and raising his arms toward heaven (a few *pentimenti* in

Fig. 25　The Angel in the Sun.
*Toledo, Ohio, Toledo Museum of Art, Gift of
Edward Drummond Libby.*

the position of the raised arms); on the right is an unidentified fragmentary sketch. The left section of the Morgan drawing is a first idea for the painting of the "Angel in the Sun Assembling the Birds of the Air, before the Destruction of the Old Beast" listed in "A Correct Catalogue of the Works of Benjamin West, Esq." in the *Supplement to La Belle Assemblée*, p. 14; there it was stated that it was "painted for William Beckford, Esq. of Fonthill." The Morgan study is closely related to the beautiful finished drawing at the Toledo Museum of Art, Toledo, Ohio, which is identified by an inscription on the verso in Benjamin West, Jr.'s, hand, as *The Angel in the Sun* (Fig. 25).

William Beckford commissioned West to paint four pictures from Revelation (see statement of account dated 30 September 1799 at the Historical Society of Pennsylvania, Philadelphia, originally sent by West to Beckford's steward, Nicholas Williams; Galt, *Life*, folio ed., III, p. 69, insert). West charged £630 for two of the pictures and £840 for the remaining two. It also appears that West had received more than half the amount due him for

these pictures in September 1799; the conclusion may therefore be drawn that two of the pictures were completed at that time.

The sale catalogue of William Beckford's collection (*Magnificent Effects at Fonthill Abbey, Wilts. to be sold by Mr. Christie on the Premises, . . . September 17, 1822, and eight following days*; the sale actually took place 1–11 October 1822) mentions "A Subject from the Revelations—very grand and spirited" (26) and "A Ditto, the companion" (27) on page 53. One may perhaps assume that the painting of the *Angel in the Sun*, which is now lost, was among these subjects and that the companion piece is the picture "of the mighty Angel, one foot upon Sea, and the other on Earth" (Revelation x, 5–8) also listed in the *Supplement to La Belle Assemblée* of 1808 on page 14. This picture dated 1798, which was exhibited at the Royal Academy in the same year (no. 76), is now in the possession of Mrs. Linden T. Harris, Drexel Hill, Pennsylvania (see Evans, *West*, pp. 60–61, pl. 41, captioned "The Archangel Gabriel"). The records of the Royal Academy mention that it was intended for the new abbey at Fonthill and the description in the Beckford sale catalogue as "very grand and spirited" surely applies to this composition. In this painting as in the Morgan study, an angel with large wings stands amid swirling clouds in front of a large luminous disk.

William Beckford was fascinated by the Book of Revelation. In fact, he envisaged his own tomb in a "Revelation Chamber" at Fonthill Abbey, which was to be hung "with the gruesome pictures in which West illustrated scenes from the sixth chapter of the Book of Revelation" (B. Alexander, *England's Wealthiest Son*, London, 1962, p. 160). Farington in his diary entry of 8 December 1798 (I, p. 251) refers to this project: "It is understood that West is to proceed painting for Mr. Beckford to the amount of £1000 a year."

60

Sketches for Windows at Fonthill Abbey
1970.11:127   PLATE 39

Black chalk. 9⅛ x 7⅚ inches (233 x 185 mm.). Irregular left margin. Several stains. Verso: Four similar sketches in black chalk. Watermark: Portal & Co. (Churchill, p. 52).

These sketches can be related to the designs for the windows at Fonthill Abbey on the basis of their elongated rectangular frames that can also be found in the finished drawing of St. Margaret, Queen of Scotland, with two male saints, in the collection of the Friends Historical Library, Swarthmore College (P.P. 257, C-1). The records of the Royal Academy exhibitions include a cartoon of St. Margaret "for a painted window in the new abbey at Fonthill." The rough sketch of a female saint at the upper right on the verso of the Morgan sheet as well as the bishop saint, possibly St. Thomas-à-Becket, at the lower left also seem to support the connection with the Fonthill Abbey windows. There is a finished drawing of St. Thomas-à-Becket at the William Rockhill Nelson Gallery of Art, Kansas City, Missouri, and a large painting of the same subject signed and dated *B. West 1797* at the Toledo Museum of Art (Acc. No. 59.32). Finally, the watermark of the paper of the drawing that Churchill connects with a date of 1796 links the sketches with this particular project. The glass-painter James P. Pearson (c 1750–1805) transferred West's design in chiaroscuro onto the glass (see Millard F. Rogers, Jr., "Benjamin West and the Caliph: two paintings for Fonthill Abbey," *Apollo*, 83, June 1966, p. 423).

The representation of a winged figure carrying a child which appears in five sketches on both sides of the Morgan sheet is, as Dr. John Plummer pointed out, a theme from Revelation XII. "The woman clothed with the sun, and the moon under her feet, and upon her head a crown of twelve stars . . . brought forth a man child. . . . And to the woman were given two wings of a great eagle, that she might fly into the wilderness. . . ." The lights shining through the windowpane behind the figure, as indicated in one of the more developed sketches on the verso, must have produced the effect desired by the artist of a woman clothed with the sun.

The picture "The Woman cloathed [sic] with the sun fleeth from the persecution of the dragon. For the new abbey at Fonthill" was exhibited at the Royal Academy in 1798 (no. 232). The *Supplement to La Belle Assemblée* of 1808 also lists a picture of "the Women [sic] clothed in the Sun" as "painted for, and in the possession of William Beckford, Esq. of Fonthill." The fate of the painting, however, is unknown.

61

Death of Hippolytus
1970.11:26

Pen and brown ink. 7⅜ x 9⅛ inches (188 x 230 mm.). Watermark: TS . . . 1799.

Both early catalogues of West's works, the *Supplement to La Belle Assemblée* of 1808 (p. 19) as well as Galt's list of West's works appended to his biography (II, p. 232), mention "The large drawing of the Death of Hippolytus" but no painting of the subject. Since the fate of the large drawing is unknown, it is fortunate that West's ideas for the composition survive in this and the following preliminary sketch. The present drawing depicts the moment when Hippolytus, driving at full speed along the narrow part of the Isthmus, was thrown from his chariot, his horses having been suddenly frightened by a huge wave rolling shoreward with a white bull springing from its crest, "bellowing and spouting water." This violent death was Hippolytus' punishment for his incestuous love for his stepmother, Phaedra (see Robert Graves, *The Greek Myths*, Baltimore, 1955, I, p. 357).

62

Death of Hippolytus
1970.11:213

Pen and brown ink. Irregular upper and left margins. 6⅝ x 8 inches (168 x 204 mm.). Watermark: Fragment of Britannia.

Hippolytus is represented amidst the pieces of his broken chariot, raising his arms in a vain effort to prevent the horses from trampling him to death. The drawing style of this and the preceding sheet with their heavy, blotting pen strokes and the rough outline of figure and horses is similar to that in the drawing *The Triumph of Nelson after the Battle of the Nile* at the Detroit Institute of Arts, which is signed and dated 1798.

63

Sibyl
1970.11:187   PLATE 37

Pen and black ink, brush and black and gray wash, heightened with white body color, on gray paper. 8¾ x 6⅝ inches (223 x 167 mm.). Verso: Drapery study in black chalk, heightened with white. Watermark: None.

This and the following drawing may represent Lady Hamilton posing as a Sibyl. Gavin Hamilton (1723–98), the Scottish painter, archaeologist, and art dealer who resided in Rome and with whom West became acquainted during his stay in Italy in 1760–63, portrayed Lady Hamilton in Naples in 1786. Two of Hamilton's paintings included in the Lady Hamilton exhibition at Kenwood in 1972 show the famous beauty in the pose of a Sibyl and of Hebe (see P. Jaffé, *Lady Hamilton in Relation to the Art of Her Time*, The Arts Council of Great Britain, Iveagh Bequest, Kenwood, 1972, nos. 34 and 35, pls. II and III). The profile and antique dress of the woman in the Morgan drawing are not unlike those of Lady Hamilton as Hebe (*op. cit.*, pl. III), a painting West could have known in the engraving after it by Domenico Cunego, or he could have drawn her from life. He certainly made her acquaintance when Sir William and Lady Hamilton as well as Lord Nelson were invited to a gala "housewarming" party at Fonthill Abbey (the new building was nearly completed) in December 1800; there Emma Hamilton sang "in her expressive and triumphant manner" and posed as Agrippina bearing the ashes of Germanicus. Benjamin West and James Wyatt, the architect, were both present at the festivities which continued far into the night (Guy Chapman, *Beckford*, London, 1952, pp. 270–73).

Both Hamilton's and West's Sibyls reveal the influence of the Bolognese *seicento*, especially of Guercino (see Thos. Agnew and Sons Ltd., *England and the Seicento*, 1973, no. 37, cover illus.).

The drapery study on the verso of the Morgan drawing may be a detail for the costume of the woman on the recto.

64

Woman in a Turban
1970.11:227

Pen and brown ink. 7 x 4½ inches (179 x 115 mm.). Irregular left margin. Watermark: None.

Like that above, this drawing may represent Lady Hamilton posing as a Sibyl. Here she is wearing a turban as in Gavin Hamilton's painting *Lady Hamilton as a Sibyl*, now in the possession of Mr. and Mrs. Clovis Whitfield, London (Jaffé, *op. cit.*, no. 34, pl. II). As in the preceding drawing, the subject is depicted in meditation, the fingers of her right hand inserted between the pages of the book in front of her.

65

The Three Marys at the Sepulchre
1970.11:84   PLATE 15

Pen and brown ink, brown wash. 4⅛ x 3¼ inches (104 x 83 mm.). Border in brown wash on old mount. Laid down. Signed in black chalk at lower right: *B. West.*

This attractive small wash drawing is an interpretation of Luke XXIV, 3–6, since it shows two figures inside Christ's tomb in accordance with the text ". . . behold, two men stood by them [the three women] in shining garments." It is perhaps a compositional sketch for the painting *The Women at the Sepulchre of Jesus Christ* which was exhibited at the Royal Academy in 1800 (no. 74). The *Supplement to La Belle Assemblée* mentions the small picture "of the Women looking into the Sepulchre, and beholding two Angels where the Lord lay" (p. 18); it was in West's own gallery in 1808. The fate of the painting is not known. The artist made very effective use of light and shade in this drawing.

66

Design for a Pediment
1970.11:126

Graphite. 7⅜ x 9 inches (188 x 229 mm.). Executed on letter paper inscribed in pen and brown ink: *Benjⁿ West Esqʳ Newman Sᵗ* Seal. Verso: Black chalk sketch of running nude man. Watermark: J. Whatman.

The Morgan sketch may be compared to the *Design for a Pediment Commemorating the Victories of Lord Howe* at the Henry E. Huntington Library and Art Gallery, San Marino, California (67.19; pen and ink and graphite, 8 x 12½ inches. Fig. 26). The latter shows the English naval hero, holding a sword in his hand, being crowned with a laurel wreath by a winged figure of Victory. The lion of Britannia lies at his feet on the left and two plaques bearing the names of his major victories can be seen on the right. The coronet and ermine perhaps signify the earldom bestowed on him in 1788. Lord Howe died in 1799.

In the Morgan design, it is Britannia who crowns the hero who appears in the nude, holding his sword in his left hand and a trident in his right. A winged figure appears to the left of him and the British lion is distinguishable in the acute angle of the triangle behind Britannia. If the word inscribed on the base of the pediment is correctly read *Rodney*, as Mr. P. van der Merwe of the National Maritime Museum, Greenwich, England, kindly suggested, West's design may have been intended for a monument honoring Admiral Sir George Brydges Rodney (1719–92). Lord Rodney was responsible in 1782 for the naval victory in the Battle of the Iles des Saintes, West Indies, during the American Revolutionary War. It is interesting to note that John Flaxman also made several sketches for a memorial to Lord Rodney (see Sotheby sale of 26 March 1975, p. 82, Lot 142, not illus.). The Flaxman drawing is described as showing Rodney as a classical victor flanked by two allegorical figures supporting a wreath which is inscribed *Jamaica*.

The frightened nude male figure, on the verso, in precipitate flight, recalls the figure of Lear in *King Lear in the Storm* at the Museum of Art, Rhode Island School of Design, Providence, and the figures in *The Grecian Daughter Defending Her Father* at the Newark Museum, Newark, New Jersey.

67

Belisarius Recognized by His Soldiers
1970.11:71   PLATE 40

Pen and brown ink. 6⁵⁄₁₆ x 7⅛ inches (160 x 182 mm.). Watermark: None.

This sketch illustrates the story of Emperor Justinian's great general who, fallen from grace, was reduced to begging for alms in his old age; he is being assisted by a young boy who felt compassion for the blind old warrior. There is another drawing of this subject, signed and dated 1784, at the Philadelphia Museum of Art (Detroit Institute of Arts / Philadelphia Museum of Art, "Romantic Art in Britain," 1968, pp. 99–100, no. 50). It shows only the two figures of the blind Belisarius in beggar's

Fig. 26   Design for a Pediment Commemorating the Victories of Lord Howe. *San Marino, California, Henry E. Huntington Library and Art Gallery.*

dress and the compassionate boy who led him through the streets of Constantinople. West's painting *Belisarius and the Boy* at the Detroit Institute of Arts (Evans, *West*, pp. 91, 97, pl. 68), which F. Cummings identified in the entry of the Detroit exhibition catalogue as the picture exhibited at the Royal Academy in 1802 under no. 139, also shows only the two figures. The blind Belisarius holding a staff is seated in the shadow of a temple; the boy standing beside him holds a round bowl, most likely a helmet, in which to collect the alms, and a sign with the inscription: *Date Obolum Belisario.*

The Morgan Library's drawing differs from the above compositions. It represents the moment depicted in Jacques-Louis David's painting of the Belisarius story in the museum at Lille, dated 1781 (R. Cantinelli, *David*, Paris and Brussels, 1930, pl. 30), when the old general is recognized by one of his soldiers while a woman is handing a coin to the boy. The group on the right in the Library's drawing, however, consists of three soldiers and the woman. Belisarius, his head and shoulders covered by a drapery, the staff in his right hand, is seated on an antique sarcophagus next to the entrance arch of a building.

John Galt, West's biographer, lists four representations of the Belisarius story in the catalogue of West's works (Appendix II, pp. 216–34), among them two small pictures of *Belisarius and the Boy*, one executed for Sir Francis Baring, the English financier and banker (1740–1810), and another "different from that in the possession of Sir Francis Baring." The former was sold at auction in 1848 (London, Christie and Manson, Sir Thomas Baring, Bart., June 2–3, 1848, Lot 26); its present location is unknown. Another version must have remained in the artist's possession; there is a picture of Belisarius listed under no. 8 in the Entrance Gallery of West's residence in Newman Street in the exhibition catalogue of 1823 which is perhaps identical with Lot 54 (24 x 14½ inches) in the Robins 1829 sale catalogue of West paintings. According to a notation in the margin of the Frick Library's copy of the sale catalogue, the picture was sold for twenty-five guineas to Sir Oswald Moseley.

The painting in Detroit has been identified with that exhibited at the Royal Academy in 1802 under no. 139 as it is a literal illustration of the words in the title under which it is listed in the catalogue of the Royal Academy, *Date Obolum Belisario.* The Morgan Library's drawing, which is a rough compositional sketch, may be a first idea for this or the other picture of Belisarius and the boy mentioned by Galt and probably identical with those exhibited at the Royal Academy in 1802 and 1805 under nos. 139 and 145 respectively. The composition of the latter is known from the 1811 engraving by H. Moses; it varies only slightly from that of the Detroit picture. West may have given up the horizontal composition of the Morgan drawing in favor of a vertical one in the painting and limited the composition to two figures only. The figures in the drawing are very close, indeed, to those in the Detroit picture—except that they are clothed in the painting; even the antique stone, decorated with sculpture in relief, on which Belisarius is seated, can be found in the painting. A date in the early years of the nineteenth century is accordingly suggested for the Morgan drawing.

The interest in the Belisarius theme was revived in the late eighteenth century with the publication in 1767 of Jean-François Marmontel's moralizing tale "Bélisaire." West may have been inspired by the book as is indicated by the words "Vide Marmontel" following the title *Belisarius and the Boy* in the Royal Academy catalogue of 1805 (no. 145). He also may have seen the smaller version of David's painting of the subject executed in part by Fabre and Girodet in 1784 (now in the Louvre) when he visited Paris in 1802, but the composition does not show any similarity with David's. Galt (I, p. 83) reports that West in his youth, before his departure for Italy in 1760, made a copy of Salvator Rosa's painting *Belisarius* from the engraving by Robert Strange. Later, upon seeing the original, which was then in Lord Townshend's collection at Rainham Hall, Norfolk—it was until recently in the late Sir Osbert Sitwell's collection, Renishaw Hall, Stafford, Derbyshire (L. Salerno, *Salvator Rosa*, Milan, 1963, no. 32)—"he was gratified to observe that he instinctively coloured his copy almost as faithfully as if it had been painted from the picture instead of the engraving." Since Robert Strange's engraving after Rosa's painting is dated 1764, four years after West's departure for Italy, Galt must have been mistaken as to the print which West used as a model. West's copy was probably based on an earlier engraving, possibly the one by Cristoforo dell'Acqua of 1709. In Rosa's picture Belisarius is standing, his type and dress are close to those of the figure in West's earlier drawing of the subject in the Philadelphia Museum. West may have borrowed the motif of the antique relief sculpture from Rosa's painting, but he used it in a different way, as a seat for Belisarius.

68

The Finding of Moses; Design for an Altar or Catafalque
1970.11:230

Pen and brown ink. 7⅞ x 8⅛ inches (200 x 205 mm.). Watermark: GR surmounted by crown, and date 1801.

Galt in his catalogue of West's works (*Life*, II, p. 224) as well as the *Supplement to La Belle Assemblée* of 1808 (p. 16) mentions a picture of "*Pharaoh's Daughter with the child Moses*; – Park, Esq. originally painted for General Lawrence." A painting entitled *The Finding of Moses* was sold at auction by the Parke-Bernet Galleries, New York, on 27 November 1968 (no. 178, illus., formerly A. Silberman collection), but the composition is different from that of the Morgan sketch.

69

Seated Female Nude
1970.11:163

Pen and black ink on gray paper. 6⅜ x 4¼ inches (162 x 108 mm.). Watermark: None.

This rough pen sketch of a female nude with *pentimenti* in the face may well be a preparatory drawing for Venus in West's composition *Venus Lamenting the Death of Adonis* of 1803, which has been preserved in one of H. Moses' outline engravings after West's paintings (see Moses, *op. cit.*, pl. IX). The painting was exhibited at the Royal Academy in 1804 (no. 131), but its present location—if it still exists—is unknown. This composition differs from the early painting of 1772 at the Carnegie Institute, Pittsburgh, Pennsylvania, in which Venus' grief is rather quiet and subdued compared to the goddess' emotional tearing of her hair here. The Morgan drawing shows the figure in a pose similar to that in the print, where, however, the artist showed her face in profile after the trial frontal schemes were discarded.

70

The Rider on the White Horse
Study for the *Destruction of the Beast and the False Prophet*, Minneapolis Institute of Arts, Minneapolis, Minnesota.
1970.11:171   PLATE 41

Black chalk, heightened with white, on blue-gray paper. 9¼ x 7 inches (235 x 178 mm.). Verso: Compositional sketch in black chalk. Watermark: Fleur-de-lis.

Like the sketch for *Death on a Pale Horse* (Cat. No. 39), this drawing is related to one of the paintings of the Revelation Dispensation for the King's Chapel in Windsor Castle. The *Supplement to La Belle Assemblée* of 1808 lists six paintings in this category, all six by eight feet in size, among them: "Saints Prostrating Themselves before the Throne of God," "The Overthrow of the Old Beast and False Prophet," and the "Last Judgment." As far as is known today, of these three only "The Overthrow of the Old Beast," also referred to as the "Destruction of the Beast and the False Prophet," has survived in the oil sketch at Minneapolis (oil on canvas, 39 x 56½ inches), which is signed and dated *B. West 1804*. However, two of the Morgan Library's drawings discussed in the following entries perhaps may convey an idea of the other two compositions cited above.

Although the Minneapolis painting has been referred to in some of the Museum's publications as "Death on a Pale Horse," it really is, as Fiske Kimball already pointed out ("Benjamin West au Salon de 1802," *Gazette des Beaux-Arts*, VII, 1932, pp. 409–10, fig. 4) an illustration of Revelation XIX, 11 and 20. The painting—most likely the large version—was exhibited at the Royal Academy in 1804 (no. 30); the small painting in Minneapolis is probably identical with Lot 38 (p. 14) in George Robins' sale catalogue of 1829. The Morgan Library's drawing shows the principal figure of the painting, the rider on the white horse wearing "many crowns" and charging into battle against the beast and the false prophet, symbols of evil.

71

*The Throne of God in Heaven and The Book
Sealed with Seven Seals* (Revelation IV–V)

1970.11:31   PLATE 42

Black and white chalk, on blue-gray paper. 6¼ x 5
inches (160 x 128 mm.). Watermark: None.

This and the following drawing seem to be part of
a group of scenes from Revelation to which the
Rider on the White Horse of the preceding entry also
belongs. All three sketches are executed in the
same medium and, as interpretations of visions from
Revelation, they are linked iconographically. The
present drawing is a precise illustration of the text
"And I saw in the right hand of him that sat on the
throne a book written within and on the backside,
sealed with seven seals. And I saw a strong angel
proclaiming with a loud voice. . . ." "The rainbow
round about the throne" and the symbols of the
evangelists at the foot of the throne are clearly
visible. The figure of the angel is reminiscent of the
Angel in the Sun (No. 59).

72

Sketch for a Last Judgment (Revelation
XX, 11–15)

1970.11:62   PLATE 43

Black and white chalk, on blue-gray paper. 5 15⁄16 x 11 ⅞
inches (150 x 301 mm.). Watermark: None.

This drawing illustrates the passage in Revelation
XX, 11–15: "And I saw a great white throne and
him that sat on it, from whose face the earth and
the heaven fled away. . . ." The figures of the
Blessed assisted by angels can be distinguished on
the left while on the right the Damned are "cast
into the lake of fire."

73

Fall of the Rebel Angels (?)

1970.11:42   PLATE 44

Black chalk, on two sheets of paper, originally pinned
together by the artist but now hinged together. 9 x
15⅛ inches (230 x 383 mm.). Squared for transfer.

Fig. 27   Thetis Bringing the Armor to Achilles.
Private Collection.

Verso: Slight sketch of a family group. Watermarks:
G R 1804 and coat-of-arms, the so-called Vryheit
(close to Heawood 3150).

This dramatic compositional sketch may be subject to various interpretations. Perhaps the title
suggested above is the most convincing one. God
the Father, seated in radiance in the clouds, is
hurling thunderbolts against an army of rebel angels falling through space at the lower right. He is
assisted by a soldier in antique battle dress with
plumed helmet and large round shield, possibly St.
Michael, standing in a defiant pose, at right. A
good angel, one holding a palm frond, can be seen
on God's right. St. Michael is similar to the figure
studies for Achilles of about the same period (Nos.
85–86).

74

Thetis Bringing the Armor to Achilles

1970.11:58   PLATE 45

Fig. 28 Thetis Bringing the Armor to Achilles. *New Britain, Connecticut, New Britain Museum of American Art, Steven Lawrence Fund.*

Black chalk. 4½ x 3½ inches (114 x 90 mm.). Bordered in black chalk. Watermark: NS.

The Morgan Library has eight drawings relating to *Thetis Bringing the Armor to Achilles*, and another five which illustrate another episode of Book XIX of the *Iliad*.

This compositional sketch is perhaps a first idea for the small painting, now in a private collection, which is signed and dated 1804 (oil on canvas, 26 x 20 inches. Fig. 27). I am indebted to Professor Helmut von Erffa for this information.

In 1805, two different painted versions of this theme were exhibited at the Royal Academy (nos. 139 and 151). The quotations from Book XIX of Alexander Pope's translation of the *Iliad*, which Graves has added in italics in his dictionary of contributors to the Royal Academy of Arts (London, 1906, IV, p. 218) next to the titles of the individual paintings, help to distinguish the two versions and the relevant drawings. The present drawing is perhaps an interpretation of verses 13–14: "Behold what arms by Vulcan are bestowed, Arms worthy thee or fit to grace a God"; the drawing discussed in the following entry illustrates verse 25: "Goddess (he cry'd) these glorious Arms that shine."

Achilles mourning the death of his comrade in arms, Patroclus, is seated on his friend's bier or bed when he is visited by his mother Thetis. West chose to represent the moment when Thetis, clad in a transparent gown, approaches and points to the armor which seems to be drifting down amid swirling clouds. There is another compositional drawing (pen and ink, 7¾ x 7 inches) for the above painting, at the New Britain Museum of American Art (formerly Bernard Black Gallery, cat. no. 15, ex Rosalie Margary collection. Fig. 28). Instead of the high-waisted dress she wears in the Morgan drawing, Thetis appears as in the painting, seminude, a veil-like drapery covering the lower part of her body.

75

Study for the Figure of Achilles
1970.11:59   PLATE 48

Black chalk. 9⅝ x 7 5/16 inches (245 x 187 mm.). Stain on upper margin. Watermark: G R 1804.

This and the following three drawings are preparatory sketches for the figure of Achilles in two oil sketches of *Thetis Bringing the Armor to Achilles*, one at the New-York Historical Society, the other at the Vassar College Art Gallery, and in the painting of the same subject at the New Britain Museum of American Art, New Britain, Connecticut. The oil sketch at the New-York Historical Society (oil on paper mounted on canvas, 17½ x 14 inches) is signed and dated 1805; the painting in New Britain (19½ x 26½ inches) is signed and dated 1806 (Fig. 32).

The *Supplement to La Belle Assemblée* of 1 July 1808 mentions on page 19 two pictures that West painted for the author and collector of antique sculpture and vases Thomas Hope: "Thetis bringing the armour from Vulcan to her son Achilles" and "Iris bearing Jove's command to King Priam, to go and solicit the body of his son Hector." On page 20 there is a reference to "the small picture of Thetis bringing the armour to Achilles in which the Myrmidons are introduced. Two sketches of the same subject without the Myrmidons—one in colours, the other in claro-scuro, in the possession of Mr. West." The painting described in the first sentence is undoubtedly the painting at the New

Britain Museum of American Art since its composition includes on the left a group of Myrmidons (the name for Achilles' subjects in Homer's *Iliad*). The painting is possibly also identical with Lot 20 on page 9 of George Robins' 1829 sale catalogue of West paintings. The other two paintings of the subject listed in the 1829 sale catalogue differ in size from the oil sketches at the New-York Historical Society and the Vassar College Art Gallery. A cartoon for the large painting which is signed and dated *B West 1805* is preserved at the Royal Academy (oil on canvas, 97 x 71 inches. Fig. 29). *Iris Bearing Jove's Command to King Priam*, the companion piece to *Thetis Bringing the Armor to Achilles*, was exhibited at the Royal Academy in 1808 (no. 63) and at the British Institution in 1809 (no. 170). There was a painting of this subject at French and Company in New York several years ago (James Thomas Flexner, *America's Old Masters*, rev. ed., 1967, pl. opp. p. 92) for which the Friends Historical Library, Swarthmore College, owns a sheet of preparatory sketches, including, on the verso, a sketch for *Thetis Bringing the Armor to Achilles* (P.P. 203; pen and brown ink, 6$\frac{15}{16}$ x 11$\frac{1}{4}$ inches; Fig. 30). Two engravings, one by William Bond, pub-

Fig. 29   Thetis Bringing the Armor to Achilles. Cartoon. *London, Royal Academy.*

Fig. 30   Thetis Bringing the Armor to Achilles (Verso of P.P. 203). *Swarthmore, Pennsylvania, Swarthmore College, Friends Historical Library.*

[45]

lished in 1809, and the other by H. Moses, published in 1811, were dedicated to Thomas Hope.

Thetis Bringing the Armor to Achilles, as illustrated in the oil sketches and paintings mentioned above, is one of West's most important neo-classical compositions. He displays an almost encyclopedic knowledge of classical armor and ornament. His keen interest in the classical decor is manifest in a large sheet of sketches at the Sabin Galleries, London (pen and ink, 185 x 235 mm.), which includes the complete design on the sheath of Achilles' sword and various ornaments on other pieces of his accoutrements. Achilles, who has been conceived in accordance with the description in Book XIX, verses 21–22, of Pope's *Iliad* translation, "From his fierce Eye-balls living Flames expire, And flash incessant like a Stream of Fire," has been acclaimed as a typical example of the "Dread Manner." West also seems to be indebted for certain details to the sculptor John Flaxman, whose outline drawings illustrating the *Iliad* were published in London in 1805. West's representation of Thetis is very similar to the goddess on plate 27 of Flaxman's *Iliad* illustrations; the ornament circling the shield and the decoration of the helmet with a winged horse also seem to come from this source.

76

Thetis Bringing the Armor to Achilles
1970.11:89   PLATES 46 AND 47

Black chalk. 9⅛ x 6⅞ inches (230 x 174 mm.). Verso: Compositional sketch in black chalk. Watermark: Buttanshaw.

The two sketches on the recto of this sheet seem to be variants of the drawing at the New Britain Museum of American Art (Fig. 28). That at the top shows Thetis gesturing toward the armor displayed at her feet. In the compositional sketch below, the goddess appears holding the shield with her left hand. Achilles and the dead Patroclus are only lightly indicated on the left. The sketch on the verso of this sheet, however, relates to a different version of the subject illustrating Book XIX, verse 25, of Pope's translation of the *Iliad*. This version may be preserved in a lithograph at the British Museum inscribed *B. West P.R.A. pinxit, Drawn on stone by H. Corbould; published by F. Moser 1 March*

1820 (38-4-25-72; 12 x 8⅞ inches. Fig. 31). Achilles, in the Morgan drawing and in the print, has leapt up, brandishing a sword in his raised right hand (the left hand in the print). Thetis, seminude, approaches with the shield from left (from the right in the lithograph).

Fig. 31   HENRY CORBOULD.
Thetis Bringing the Armor to Achilles.
Lithograph.
London, British Museum.

77

Thetis Bringing the Armor to Achilles
1970.11:91

Black chalk. 5 x 14⅝ inches (126 x 372 mm.). Slightly irregular upper margin; formerly folded in center. Watermark: Coat-of-arms with horn surmounted by crown and date 1802.

Two of the sketches on these leaves may also be connected with the small painting in a private collection (Fig. 27); the other two show the composition in the opposite direction and therefore may be linked to the important painting in the

New Britain Museum of American Art of 1806 (Fig. 32) where Achilles and the body of Patroclus are placed on the right and Thetis is seen approaching from the left. Another sheet of related sketches is at the Vassar College Art Gallery, Poughkeepsie, New York (black crayon, 6 x 9¾ inches, inscribed in pen and ink at upper left, *B. West Esq.*; Bernard Black Gallery cat. no. 16. Here Fig. 33).

academic drawing book intended for the use of Royal Academy students, of which there is a copy at the Print Room, Metropolitan Museum of Art, New York (Acc. No. 60. 653. 15, Gift of Lincoln Kirstein; *Elements of Drawing in a Series of Examples Extracted from Pictures By*, and in the Gallery of, *Benjamin West, Esq.*, engraved by Edward Scriven and published by T. Clay, London, 1813, pl. 7).

See No. 75.

78

Study for the Legs of Achilles
1970.11:185   PLATE 49

Black chalk, heightened with white, on gray paper. 8¾ x 11¼ inches (223 x 286 mm.). Watermark: None,

It is interesting to note that the legs of Achilles in this drawing appear in reverse direction in an

79

Study for the Right Leg and Drapery of Achilles
1970.11:90   PLATE 49

Black chalk. 9⅛ x 6⅞ inches (232 x 165 mm.). Watermark: GR 1804.

See No. 75.

Fig. 32   Thetis Bringing the Armor to Achilles. Painting.
New Britain, Connecticut, New Britain Museum of American Art, Charles F. Smith Fund.

80

Design for a Helmet
1970.11:87   PLATE 50

Pen and brown ink over indications in graphite. 8¼ x 6¾ inches (206 x 172 mm.). Watermark: C Wilmott 1803.

The design of a helmet has been incorporated unchanged into the cartoon and the painted versions of *Thetis Bringing the Armor to Achilles*. As already mentioned, it may have been inspired by Flaxman's *Iliad* illustrations (Mars' helmet in *The Gods Descending into Battle*, pl. 32). Another somewhat less elaborate drawing of a helmet (pen and ink, 235 x 187 mm.) at the Sabin Galleries, London, may have been intended for one of Achilles' soldiers in the painting at the New Britain Museum of American Art.

See No. 75.

81

Studies for the Figure of Achilles
1970.11:92   PLATE 56

Black chalk. 5¼ x 6 inches (130 x 152 mm.). Irregular upper margin, upper part of sheet and lower right corner torn off, several creases. Verso: Receipt in pen and ink dated . . . *July 1793* and signed by Francis Seaman. Watermark: None.

On this sheet of sketches West studied various poses for Achilles; the more developed one on the right is similar to that in the paintings mentioned in the preceding entries.

82

Achilles Wearing the Armor Brought by Thetis
1970.11:60   PLATE 52

Pen and brown ink. 9⅞ inches x 8⅛ inches (252 x 206 mm.). Red seal at lower right. Verso: Invitation (printed except for name and address which are written by hand) addressed to *Benjamin West Esq | Newman Street* to attend the quarterly general meeting of the Governors and Guardians of The Foundling Hospital on 30 December 1807 at one o'clock (West was a Governor of the Foundling Hospital). Watermark: None.

This sheet includes two compositional sketches which more or less repeat the concept represented in the preceding drawing, and three studies of the principal figure Achilles. He is shown here in full armor as described by the poet in the *Iliad*, Book XIX, verses 400–11: "the brazen Sword a various Baldrick ty'd, / that, starr'd with Gems, hung glitt'ring at his side; / And like the Moon, the broad refulgent Shield . . . Next, his high Head the Helmet grac'd; behind / the sweepy Crest hung floating in the Wind. . . ." Here in this drawing, Achilles is shown holding a spear in accordance with verses 420–21 "And now he shakes his great paternal Spear, / Pond'rous and huge! which not a *Greek* could rear."

83

Achilles Mourning the Death of Patroclus
1970.11:233   PLATE 53

Pen and brown ink. 9¼ x 7⅟₁₆ inches (235 x 180 mm.). Red seal at left center. Verso: Another sketch in pen and brown ink on paper inscribed *B West Esqr | Newman Street*. Watermark: Several numerals (perhaps 1810).

This is another sheet of sketches which includes a compositional drawing on the recto, another on the verso, and several studies of Achilles at the bier of Patroclus along with a number of studies of Achilles alone in various attitudes of grief.

The compositional sketch on the recto shows Achilles seated in front of Patroclus' bier holding his new armor; the other mourners are gathered at the foot and head of the bier. The compositional sketch on the verso seems to represent the episode when the Greek leaders, among them Agamemnon and Ulysses, came to Achilles, pleading with him to rejoin the battle, and Achilles asks their forbearance until sunset so that he may devote another day of mourning to his dead friend. The group of the Greek leaders appears on the right, their ships summarily indicated in the distance behind them.

Fig. 33   Thetis Bringing the Armor to Achilles. Sheet of Sketches.
Poughkeepsie, New York, Vassar College Art Gallery.

84

Achilles Wearing the Armor Brought by Thetis

1970.11:232   PLATE 54

Pen and brown ink. 5⅜ x 5¼ inches (141 x 134 mm.).
Laid down.

This and the following four drawings may be related to Book XIX, verses 295–325 and 390–425, of
Pope's translation of the *Iliad*. In order to soothe
Achilles' anger and induce him to rejoin the battle
against the Trojans, Agamemnon returned Briseis,
the beautiful maiden whom he had taken from
Achilles as compensation for Chryseis, whom Agamemnon had had to give up (see No. 16). Briseis
and her "sister captives" here are seen mourning
the dead Patroclus while the helmeted Achilles,
carrying a large, round shield, is ready to sally
forth into combat on the side of the Greeks. It appears from the drawing that West drew Briseis and
the women at the bier first and then superimposed
the towering figure of the hero, who is prominently
placed in the foreground.

Although the records of the Royal Academy as
well as those of the British Institution give no clue
to any painting illustrating the above scene, this
and the following four drawings suggest that West
perhaps considered executing one or two more
paintings illustrating the *Iliad* to add to *Thetis
Bringing the Armor to Achilles* and *Iris Delivering
Jove's Command to Priam*.

85

Study for the Figure of Achilles

1970.11:79   PLATE 51

Pen and brown ink, over slight landscape drawing in
graphite. 5¾ x 4⅛ inches (147 x 105 mm.). Verso:
Fragmentary sketch in black chalk. Watermark: G R
1804.

This and the following pen sketch of a classical
warrior posed with spear and shield may be further studies for Achilles. The ornament bordering
the shield is the same as that in the Royal Academy cartoon and in the paintings of Thetis.

See No. 82.

86

Study for the Figure of Achilles

1970.11:88   PLATE 55

Pen and brown ink. 7¼ x 4¾ inches (185 x 120 mm.). Watermark: G R 1804.

West altered the pose of Achilles from the preceding drawing by showing his head in frontal rather than profile view and by placing his left foot on an elevated platform, thus giving the figure a *contrapposto* balance. There are *pentimenti* in the right arm holding the spear and the right leg.

See No. 82.

87

Midshipman's Berth and Cockpit Ladder of the "Victory"
Preparatory sketch for the painting *The Death of Nelson*, National Maritime Museum, Greenwich England.

1970.11:223   PLATE 57

Pen and black ink, gray wash. 9 x 12⅛ inches (228 x 307 mm.). Irregular margins. Inscribed in black chalk by the artist: *Midshipman's Birth & Cockpit Ladder as seen from the Cable tiers.* Watermark: Coat-of-arms of England (close to Churchill 217).

The Battle of Trafalgar was fought on 21 October 1805. Joseph Farington reports in his diary on 4 December 1805 that "The Victory arrived at Portsmouth with the remains of Lord Nelson." Lord Nelson's funeral took place on 6 January 1806. Farington further states on 5 May 1806 that when he called on West, "He was seated before His new finished picture of 'The Death of Lord Nelson.' " Although the picture at Greenwich, which shows the hero of Trafalgar dying in the hold of the *Victory*, is signed and dated *B. West 1808* (see G. Evans, *West*, pp. 89, 100, pl. 65) and was exhibited in that year at the Royal Academy (no. 119), we must assume that West worked on the project of a Nelson monument for a period of several years, probably from December 1805 onward when Lord Hawkesbury, the Secretary of State, communicated the King's command to the members of the Royal Academy "to consider the

best mode of perpetuating the memory of Lord Nelson." Besides the picture just mentioned, West executed *The Apotheosis of Nelson* of 1807, for which there is a sketch in the Mellon Collection, London, and the *Death of Lord Nelson*, 1811, where the scene is set on the quarterdeck of the *Victory*, now at the Walker Art Gallery, Liverpool. In the *Supplement to La Belle Assemblée* of July 1808 on page 20, two pictures are mentioned, *The Death of Lord Nelson in the Cockpit of "The Victory"* and *Victory Bearing the Body of Lord Nelson* . . . (i.e., *The Apotheosis of Nelson*), which were originally painted by West for John MacArthur, the author in collaboration with James S. Clarke of *The Life of Lord Nelson*; they may be identical with the two paintings of the same subjects now at the Greenwich National Maritime Museum. Despite the careful preparation manifest in the Morgan drawing, West failed to make significant use of the details of this interior view in the Greenwich painting.

88

The Bard

1970.11:251   PLATE 58

Black chalk on red-ruled paper. 5 3/16 x 3½ inches (131 x 89 mm.). Border in gray wash on old mat. Watermark: None.

This and the following two drawings are preparatory sketches for West's painting *The Bard* which was exhibited at the Royal Academy in 1809 (no. 119) and at the British Institution in 1811 (no. 29). It was inspired by Thomas Gray's Pindaric ode of the same title written in 1755–57. The painting exhibited at the Royal Academy in 1809 was included as Lot 42 of the Raphael West sale (George Robins, *A Catalogue of Nine Pictures of the First Class; the genuine Property of Mr. Raphael West*, 16 July 1831); these nine pictures, "the last relic of the valuable Gallery of Benjamin West, Esq," consisted of four old masters and five of Benjamin West's own paintings, among them *The Bard*. The compiler of the sale catalogue speaks of the unqualified applause the picture received from contemporary painters and describes the reaction of the famous actress Mrs. Siddons to the painting when she saw it upon its completion in West's studio. She immediately recited the line from *The*

Bard "Ruin seize thee ruthless king!" and further commented, "had the poet been the painter of the Bard, he must have painted it thus."

West's composition of *The Bard* has been preserved in an engraving by John Charles Bromley, Jr. (1795–1839), of which there is an impression at the British Museum (Vol. III, Case 22, p. 5. Fig. 34). The engraving of *The Bard* is mentioned in a letter of 16 January 1815 addressed to West from William Bromley, the father of John Charles; the letter which is preserved at the Historical Society of Pennsylvania (Galt, *Life*, folio ed., III, p. 103, insert), states that the plate of "the Bard, engraved by my son, . . . has not yet been printed" and thus furnishes an approximate date for the engraving.

The Morgan drawing shows essentially the same composition as the print although in the opposite direction. West, however, changed the pose of the figure. He is seen full face and violently waves both arms in the drawing; in the print, on the other hand, the bearded poet appears in profile and holds the lyre with his left hand. The stance of the

Fig. 34 JOHN CHARLES BROMLEY, JR.
The Bard. Engraving.
London, British Museum.

figure, the rocky crag, the billowing drapery, the clouds as an effective backdrop for the tall figure were retained in the print, which also shows the ravens and eagles mentioned in the poem. The drawing with its tortuous lines reflects the somber mood of the poem.

89

The Bard

1970.11:32   PLATE 59

Black chalk on blue paper. 10¾ x 17⅝ inches (272 x 440 mm.). Vertical crease in center. Verso: Three drapery studies in black chalk, heightened with white on blue paper. Watermark: None.

There are two sketches for *The Bard* on this sheet, one showing the bearded head and torso of the poet, the other outlining the whole figure almost exactly as it appears in Bromley's engraving, only the position of the arm holding the lyre being somewhat different. The fine details of drapery on the verso of this sheet hopefully may be identified in the future with those in one of West's paintings. A very slight, scarcely visible sketch of the Bard appears in the upper left corner of the sheet.

90

The Bard

1970.11:93

Pen and brown ink. 5⅜ x 4 inches (137 x 101 mm.). Laid down.

This spirited pen sketch can perhaps also be related to West's *Bard*. The pose of the lower part of the figure, here shown in the nude, as well as the fluttering drapery and billowing clouds, seem to support this assumption.

See No. 88.

91

Standing Nude Youth

1970.11:173   PLATE 60

Black chalk, heightened with white, on brown prepared paper. 11¼ x 7¼ inches (285 x 184 mm.). Watermark: None.

The slender figure of a youth draped in a transparent veil and holding an object, perhaps a torch, in his raised left hand, may be a first idea for Cupid in West's painting *Omnia Vincit Amor*, or *The Power of Love in the Three Elements*, exhibited at the Royal Academy in 1811 (no. 63) and now at the Metropolitan Museum of Art, New York (see Gardner and Feld, *op. cit.*, pp. 35–36). Cupid in the painting, however, has been given large wings and a stance taken from Laocoön as suggested in the museum's catalogue. Whatever its interpretation, the easy grace of the figure in the Morgan drawing somehow seems to evoke the spirit of late antiquity.

92

Two Women Carrying Baskets on Their Heads

1970.11:206

Black chalk on gray-brown paper. 6⅝ x 9⅝ inches (170 x 244 mm.). Verso: Compositional sketch in black chalk for a Resurrection. Watermark: None.

These two half-length figures of women carrying baskets, which West may have observed in a London street market, appear in the background of his large painting *Christ Healing the Sick in the Temple* of 1814, now at the Pennsylvania Hospital, Philadelphia, Pennsylvania (G. Evans, *West*, pl. 4). The original version was completed in March 1811 and exhibited at the British Institution in April of that year and again in 1812. An oil sketch for the picture was shown at the Royal Academy as early as 1801 (no. 307). West added fruits and leaves to one of the women's baskets in the Philadelphia painting but otherwise used this genre motif unchanged. The rough compositional sketch of the Resurrection on the verso of this sheet can perhaps be related to one of West's later versions of this subject. The records of the Royal Academy exhibitions include a sketch of the Resurrection in 1808 (no. 117) and another as late as 1819 (no. 111). One may perhaps surmise that West contemplated a large picture of the subject at this late stage in his career but did not live to complete the project. In fact, there is strong evidence that West in this last period took up many of the themes he had painted earlier, for example, the *Crucifixion* (see No. 104) and *Peter's Denial of Christ* (No. 107). In the present drawing Christ is seated on the sepulchre in the center, a group of angels approach from the left, and a frightened soldier is seen fleeing from the scene at right.

93

Allegory of Britannia

1970.11:177   PLATE 61

Pen and brown ink. 5⅝ x 5⅝ inches (144 x 143 mm.). Verso: Sketch for the same composition. Watermark: None.

The sketch on the recto of this drawing can be related to a finished pen drawing at the Henry E. Huntington Library and Art Gallery, San Marino, California (63.52.287; 9 x 5⁹⁄₁₆ inches; signed and dated *B. West 1812*. Fig. 35). There were two more sketches connected with the same project in the Bernard Black Gallery exhibition of West drawings in 1968 (E. Maurice Bloch, *op. cit.*, nos. 19 verso and 21). All three show the principal figure of Britannia (seated on a raised platform in the Morgan sketch, standing in one of the Bernard Black sheets) surrounded by Religion and other

Fig. 35   Allegory of Britannia. *San Marino, California, Henry E. Huntington Library and Art Gallery.*

figures with Christ appearing in the clouds above.

The verso of the Morgan drawing, however, may be connected with West's 1812 portrait of John Eardley Wilmot, the Commissioner appointed to adjust the claims of the American Loyalists. In the background of the portrait, which was exhibited at the Royal Academy in the year of its execution (no. 58), one sees hanging on the wall of the Commissioner's study an allegorical picture of Britannia as protectress of the Loyalists. Wilmot's portrait was included in Sotheby's sale of 18 November 1970 (no. 60, illus.). The sketch on the verso of the Morgan drawing is clearly related to this "painting within a painting" which, according to Lewis Einstein (*Divided Loyalties—Americans in England during the War of Independence*, Boston and New York, 1933, pp. 241–42), is "an allegorical sketch, now lost, in which Religion and Justice extended the mantle of Britannia which, with outstretched arms, receives the loyalists . . ." and "which was used by Wilmot as the frontispiece for his account of the work of the commission" (*Historical View of the Commission for enquiring into the losses, services, and claims of the American loyalists . . .*, London, 1815. Fig. 36). Britannia is seen in profile as on the verso of the Morgan sheet; she extends her hand toward a group of Loyalists, one of whom, an Indian chief, raises his arm in salute to Britannia. The frontispiece to the Commissioner's report, an engraving by H. Moses after West's design, includes a portrait of the artist holding a cane (he was seventy-seven years old in 1815).

94

Study for "Saul and the Witch of Endor"

Fig. 36   H. MOSES. Allegory of Britannia. Frontispiece to the Commissioner's Report Regarding Claims of the American Loyalists. *New Haven, Connecticut, Yale University Library.*

Pen, brown ink, and brown wash, over preliminary drawing in black chalk; the two figures on the right are only faintly indicated in black chalk. 7⅞ x 12½ inches (199 x 317 mm.). Stain of brown wash at upper right. Watermark: Golding & Snelgrove 1812.

The Morgan drawing, on the basis of the watermark, seems to be a later version of the subject represented in West's painting at the Wadsworth Atheneum, Hartford, Connecticut (oil on canvas, 20½ x 27 inches), which is signed and dated *B. West 1777*. A copy of the painting is preserved at the Victoria and Albert Museum (D.23-1869, Dyce collection). There is also an engraving after West's painting by William Sharp, published by J. & J. Boydell; the second state of the engraving is dated 1788.

The painting and the Morgan drawing illustrate the Old Testament story found in the first book of Samuel. Saul, threatened by an army of Philistines and anxious about his fate and that of his soldiers, visits the Witch of Endor. Upon Saul's request, she summons the spirit of the prophet Samuel who predicts doom for Saul and his host, whereupon Saul falls in shock to the ground. In the drawing, the composition of the earlier painting has been reversed. The figure of Saul in the drawing is changed somewhat from that in the earlier painting. Stretched out full length on the ground, he lifts his head slightly, terror in his eyes; in the painting he buries his head between his arms, not daring to look up at the apparition.

95

Two Sketches of a Soldier with Helmet and Shield

1970.11:186

Black chalk. 8½ x 11 inches (216 x 279 mm.). Inscribed in pen and brown ink on recto: *B West Esq | & & &.* Seal. Verso: Invitation signed by Henry Howard, Secretary of the Royal Academy, and dated 31 July 1813, requesting West to meet with the President and the members of the Council on 3 August "to proceed with the Revision of the Abstract." Watermark: John Hall.

The Greek warrior holding a large shield and wearing a helmet with waving plumes is depicted in the act of recoiling from some danger or super-

natural force, in this case the lightning of Jupiter. The figure is similar to Diomed in the painting *Diomed and His Horses Stopped by the Lightning of Jupiter* (*Iliad*, Book VIII, verses 160–76) which is signed and dated *B. West 1793* and was exhibited at J. Leger & Son, New York in 1930 (see Evans, *West*, pp. 77–78, pl. 58). A preparatory drawing for this painting is in the Boston Museum of Fine Arts (42.612; pen and brown ink, 10⅜ x 15⅞ inches); it is signed and dated *B. West 1788*.

The discrepancy in date between the Morgan sketches, with their obvious connection with the drawing of 1788 and the painting of 1793 on one hand and the invitation of 1813 on the verso of the same sheet on the other, can perhaps be resolved by hazarding the guess that West copied his own figure for a later version of the same subject. The second sketch on the Morgan sheet which shows the warrior standing on the platform of his chariot, as well as the figure beside him, seems to support this hypothesis.

96

Christ Bound
Sketch for *Christ in the Hall of Caiphas*

1970.11:216   PLATE 63

Pen and brown ink, brown and gray wash. About 6 x 2½ inches (about 153 x 62 mm.). The silhouetted figure of Christ, originally pinned to the drawing of a Roman soldier, is now hinged to the sheet. Irregular upper margin. Watermark: Golding & [Snelgrove].

This and the following two drawings can be related to West's *Christ in the Hall of Caiphas*, pre-

Fig. 37   Christ in the Hall of Caiphas.
Museum of Fine Arts, Boston, Gift in Memory of John H. Sturgis by His Daughters.

served in a compositional sketch at the Boston Museum of Fine Arts (Fig. 37). On the back of the old mount, Benjamin West, Jr., commented: *A design for a Picture which Mr. West intended to paint the size of his Christ Rejected– Benjn West* (Acc. No. 42.580; pen, brown ink, brown wash, heightened with white body color, 12½ x 18¼ inches). The drawing is undoubtedly identical with no. 27 in the 1839 sale catalogue of West drawings since the text on the title page of the catalogue clearly states: "Mr. Benjamin West, as a voucher for the authenticity of his Father's Drawings, has placed his signature at the back of each of them." The Boston drawing, incidentally, consists of at least four sections which have been combined to form one sheet; likewise, the Morgan drawing, with the silhouetted figure of Christ pinned to that of the Roman soldier, aptly demonstrates the creative process. In fact, after the pin was removed in the Morgan Library's laboratory, it became clear that Christ was first intended by the artist to stand to the right of the standing Roman legionnaire just as in the Boston drawing; the former figure was then cut from the sheet and placed to the left. There are several instances of this working method among West's drawings, for example, the British Museum drawing *Christ, the Archangel Michael, Apollyon and Angels* (198 b 10, Book of Drawings, p. 1) and the Morgan drawing (No. 100).

West, in this late period of his career, was occupied with his large, many-figured compositions. *Christ Healing the Sick* had been completed in 1811. Joseph Farington in his diary entry of 18 January 1813 notes that he had "some conversation with West respecting the great picture which He was now employed upon—Pilate shewing Christ to the Jews." This composition is preserved in a drawing *Christ before Pilate* formerly on the London art market (pencil and wash, 11⅝ x 18⅜ inches; *Apollo*, N.S. 83, March 1966, p. lxxiii), which may have been intended as a companion to *Christ in the Hall of Caiphas* or else represents an early concept of West's *Christ Rejected* of 1814.

97

Christ Bound and a Group of Soldiers
1970.11:197   PLATE 63

Black chalk. 5 x 4⅛ inches (128 x 105 mm.). Vertical

crease, right of center. Verso: Inscribed in pen and brown ink: *Benjn West Esquire.* Watermark: None.

In contrast to the Boston drawing where Christ is shown to the left of the seated soldier, he appears here on the right. The figure of Christ as well as the seated soldier with a shield can also be found in the drawing *Christ before Pilate*, formerly on the London art market. Both Christ and the standing Roman legionnaire with a pointed, plumed helmet and lance also appear almost unchanged in West's *Peter's Denial of Christ*, 1819 (No. 107).

See No. 96.

98

Christ Bound
1970.11:140

Black chalk. The head of Christ has been gone over with pen and brown ink. 6⁵⁄₁₆ x 7¹³⁄₁₆ inches (160 x 198 mm.). Inscribed by the artist in pen and brown ink on verso: *Struck at this thy greatest design.* Watermark: Snelgrove 1813.

The figure of Christ, his hands crossed and tied, is very similar to that in the preceding drawing and the Boston compositional sketch.

See No. 96.

99

Sketch for the Installation of "Christ Rejected by the Jews"
1970.11:28   PLATE 64

Pen and brown ink, on heavy oatmeal paper. 14⅜ x 20⁷⁄₁₆ inches (365 x 519 mm.). Vertical crease through center and some repairs. Watermark: None. Signed and dated: *Benjn. West Decem^r. 21st 1813-.* Inscribed in pencil by a different hand on verso: *Portfolio | with ods & ends | journals–Drawings | of mine and the childrens | M M 1856.*

Joseph Farington reports in his diary entry of 18 January 1813 (VII, p. 143) that at this time West was working on his great picture "Pilate shewing Christ to the Jews" and that this day he was offered 8,000 guineas for it. The painting, according to Whitley (*Art in England, 1800–1820*, New York, 1928, pp. 231–32), was finished in May 1814 and from June until late in autumn 1814 was on view in the Great Room, formerly the Royal Academy, 125 Pall Mall. The large painting, 34 feet in length by 16 in height and containing 120 figures, attracted thousands of visitors. (There is a discrepancy between these measurements and those given in Robins' 1829 sale catalogue, 16 feet 9 inches high by 22 feet wide, and the Pennsylvania Academy of Fine Arts catalogue of December 1843, 17 by 20 feet).

It is undoubtedly for the installation in the building in Pall Mall that West made the Morgan Library's sketch (1970.11:28). There was another sketch in pen and ink, also on heavy paper, recently on the art market (Kenneth W. Rendell, Inc., *Autograph Letters, Manuscripts, Documents*, catalogue 58, pp. 39–40, no. 169, illus.). The latter shows the side wall of the exhibition room with various draperies and a bust on a mantel as well as a profile view of the "splended frame after the model of the Gate of Theseus at Athens" mentioned by Whitley (*loc. cit.*). West attached great importance to the manner in which his paintings should be viewed. Albert Ten Eyck Gardner in his study "West's Legacy," *The Metropolitan Museum of Art Bulletin*, March 1966, pp. 225–36, reproduced a view of Benjamin West's gallery in his house in Newman Street, London. It shows a similar arrangement to that in the aforementioned drawings with draperies festooned along the walls and around the paintings, and a canopy supported by slender soaring columns in the center which was intended to diffuse the light. There are also two small domes admitting light indicated in the side view of the installation of *Christ Rejected*, one directly above the painting, the other in the center of the gallery. Gardner noted that "this dramatic and opulent style of art gallery decoration persisted through the nineteenth century, and was adopted by the Metropolitan Museum in the 1880s and 1890s."

John Sartain (*The Reminiscences of a Very Old Man*, New York, 1899, p. 232) relates the story of the painting's discovery in a London shop by the Philadelphia picture restorer Richardson and its subsequent purchase on Richardson's recommendation by Joseph Harrison, Jr., the railroad engineer, who had it sent to Philadelphia. It was exhibited at the Pennsylvania Academy of Fine Arts for the first time in December 1843 (Great Exhibition of Religious Paintings, by the Pennsylvania

Academy of the Fine Arts, at the Artists' Fund Hall, Philadelphia, 1843, no. 1).

100

Adam and Eve
1970.11:228

Pen and brown ink. The drawing has been cut in two parts and pasted onto another sheet. 8⅛ x 7¾ inches (207 x 198 mm.). Verso of drawing inscribed in pen and brown ink: *Benjamin West, Esq. | Newman Street | London*. Watermarks: On one sheet, coat-of-arms with horn and monogram (close to Heawood 2767); on the other, J. Budgen 1814.

This late drawing of a man and a woman possibly represents Adam and Eve in Paradise with the head of Satan amid the clouds at the upper right. It is perhaps an illustration of some verses of Milton's *Paradise Lost*, Book IV. The somewhat crude outline drawing of the two figures with their expressionless faces and vague gestures is a typical product of West's late period.

101

The Victory of Waterloo
1970.11:29   PLATE 65

Pen and brown ink. 6⅜ x 6⁷⁄₁₆ inches (158 x 163 mm.). Diameter of design: 4½ inches (114 mm.). Verso: Draft of a letter in the artist's hand dated 25 August 1815. Watermark: [Tur]key Mill / 1806.

This and the following two sketches as well as a finished drawing at the Art Gallery of Ontario, Toronto (Fig. 38), were executed by West to commemorate the victory at the Battle of Waterloo on 18 June 1815.

A letter from Benjamin West to Sir George Beaumont, dated 20 September 1815, contains detailed suggestions for a national monument commemorating the victory of Waterloo. The autograph letter is now at the Historical Society of Pennsylvania, Philadelphia (inserted in the folio ed. of Galt, *Life*, IV, p. 108); it was published in the small edition of Galt's biography of West (II, pp. 235–39), but there bears the date of 30 September 1815.

West's idea for a national monument never became a reality, but he obviously participated in the plans for a commemorative medal. It was perhaps in response to yet another letter, one from the Master of the Mint, William Wellesley-Pole, Earl of Mornington, dated 11 July 1815, that West executed this Morgan drawing for a Waterloo medal (see W. J. Hocking, *Royal Mint Museum Catalogue*, II, *Dies, Medals & Seals*, 1910, pp. 207–10). It appears from this letter that two medals were to be struck, "one in Gold of the largest size" to be given to each of the sovereigns of the Alliance and to their ministers and generals, the other "in Bronze of a smaller size" to be given to every officer and soldier who fought in the battle, both medals having the Prince Regent's head on the obverse. Another West letter at the Historical Society of Pennsylvania (Galt, *Life*, folio ed., IV, p. 25), dated Newman Street, 7 August 1815, and addressed to William Wellesley-Pole, refers to two medals to commemorate the Battles of Les Quatre-Bras and Waterloo, but it is John Flaxman who is mentioned as the artist unanimously chosen by the gentlemen of the Royal Academy to prepare the designs under their inspection. Flaxman's design as described by Smirke to Joseph Farington (Farington diary of 15 August 1815) showed "wisdom & Fortitude" (Minerva and Hercules) with Justice holding the balance and these figures crowned by Victory. It seems that neither West's nor Flaxman's designs were made into medals. The smaller medal was executed in silver by the medalist Thomas Wyon, Jr., in 1815. The execution of the larger medal, for which the Italian lapidary and medalist Benedetto Pistrucci was to submit a design in 1816, was protracted until 1848; the medal was never struck in gold due to the technical difficulty of hardening dies of this size (5.3 inches in diameter). Only an electrotype and two gutta-percha impressions survive along with the dies (W. J. Hocking, *op. cit.*, p. 210). (Information concerning these Waterloo medals was kindly supplied by Mr. J. S. Martin of the Department of Coins and Medals, British Museum.)

The draft of a letter on the verso of this drawing, dated 25 August 1815, introduces Charles Long, Baron Farnborough (1761–1828), and his wife to Baron Dominique Vivant Denon (1747–1825), Director-General of the museums of France, whom West had met during his stay in Paris in the fall of 1802. The actual letter, dated 29 August 1815, is at the Historical Society of Pennsylvania, Philadelphia (Galt, *Life*, folio ed., III, p. 79, insert).

102

The Victory of Waterloo
1970.11:30   PLATE 65

Pen and brown ink. $4\frac{1}{8}$ x $2\frac{13}{16}$ inches (109 x 72 mm.). Laid down. Watermark: None.

The present sketch very likely represents a first idea for the finished drawing at Toronto (*Figure of Victory*, pen and watercolor, $8\frac{3}{8}$ x $5\frac{7}{8}$ inches. Fig. 38) which, as the rectangular format suggests, might have been intended for a commemorative painting or print. The Toronto drawing as well as two of the Morgan sketches show the winged nude figure of Victory, his drapery secured by a strap across his chest, holding palm and laurel branches and a scroll inscribed *Waterloo*. As in the Toronto sheet, the figure in the Library's drawing is borne aloft on clouds above the battlefield.

Fig. 38   The Victory of Waterloo.
Art Gallery of Ontario, Toronto, Gift of Miss Joan Arnoldi, 1939.

103

Nude Youth with Drapery

1970.11:221   PLATE 65

Pen and brown ink. 5⅞ x 4⅛ inches (149 x 105 mm.). Laid down.

This sketch of a nude youth can be grouped with West's designs commemorating the victory of Waterloo. Although represented here without wings, the figure raises his arms in the same triumphant gesture as in the preceding drawing and the drapery slung over his left arm and flowing down his back is arranged in a similar manner.

See above.

104

The Crucifixion

1970.11:56   PLATE 66

Black chalk, on three pieces of oatmeal paper, originally pinned together by the artist. Some passages have been gone over with pen and brown ink. 12¹³⁄₁₆ x 23 inches (325 x 585 mm.). Inscribed in black chalk on verso: *Feb^y-5th-1814.*

This and the following two drawings can be related to the same project, a large many-figured composition of the Crucifixion. Farington in his diary entry for 22 May 1817 reports that "Mr. West, now almost 79 years old, told us that besides the great picture of 'Death on the Pale Horse,' which He now has in hand, He has upon a canvass 36 feet high, by 28 feet deep, a picture drawn in, the subject 'The Crucifixion.'" Farington further adds the remark: "He appeared to be recovered from the debility which He felt at the Annual Academy Dinner."

West, who was afflicted by the ills of old age, undoubtedly had to rely on the assistance of his son Raphael for the completion of these late large canvases. Another Farington entry dated 8 September 1815 is revealing as to the collaboration between father and son: "Ralph [sic] West told me that for ¾ of a year past he has resided near Staines, the air of that place agreing well with His wife & daugr. . . . He spoke of the assistance He gave His Father [Benjamin West] in tracing on large canvasses the subjects for which His Father made Sketches, who when He comes to paint finds

every form in its place, but nothing more than a general outline, a space for Him to fill up agreeably to His own Ideas.– thus all the tedious & dry business of preparation His Father is relieved from, besides the fatigue of doing it." This information clearly shows that the older West, in spite of the gout which at times impaired the use of his hands, remained in charge of invention and design to the very end of his life. Yet late sketches like the present drawing reveal a certain coarseness in draughtsmanship and figures reduced to mere outlines, which may be attributable to the ebbing of his physical strength.

This sketch for a Crucifixion, as compared with the earlier drawing (No. 21), is a more conventional formulation of the subject with the three crosses and the centurion on horseback on the left and the temple and other buildings crumbling under the impact of the earthquake on the right. One of the dead is seen emerging from under a large tombstone in the center foreground, next to a group of three figures, perhaps the chief priests (one of them a woman) who had mocked Christ on the cross but now huddle together in fear.

Unfortunately, the *Crucifixion* of 1796–97, the glass-painting for the central portion of the West window in St. George's Chapel, Windsor, was destroyed in a hurricane in Calcutta, and only a fragmentary study for this composition survives in the Julius S. Held collection (*Selections from the Drawing Collection of Mr. and Mrs. Julius S. Held*, Binghamton, 1970, p. 12, no. 20, illus.). Another pen and wash drawing of *Christ on the Cross* with a group of figures below the Cross, signed *B. West* (7¾ x 7 inches), in a New York private collection, is perhaps to be connected with the St. George's Chapel *Crucifixion*.

105

A Group of Witnesses of the Crucifixion

1970.11:131   PLATE 67

Graphite, pen and brown ink, over black chalk, on oatmeal paper. 8 x 7¹¹⁄₁₆ inches (204 x 195 mm.). Verso: Graphite sketch of a group of figures. Watermark: None.

On the recto of this sheet West first sketched some figures in graphite and then modified the right half of his design by pasting another sheet of paper over the original drawing. The drawing on this added sheet, executed in pen and brown ink over indications in black chalk, is a study for the central part of the composition. It shows an old man, perhaps a priest, his head covered with a cloth, tearing at his beard and a crowd of people pointing to Christ on the Cross. The drawing on the verso is a sketch for the right half of the composition. The woman viewed from the back with a child clinging to her now is seen in the company of several other figures in various attitudes of fear.

106

Christ on the Cross
1970.11:265

Black chalk on oatmeal paper. 6⅝ x 4⅝ inches (170 x 117 mm.). Irregular left margin. Watermark: None.

This summary sketch may well be a detail for the large composition of the Crucifixion as the cross and Christ's body are drawn at a similar angle as in the compositional sketch.

See No. 104.

107

Peter's Denial of Christ
1970.11:124   PLATE 68

Pen and brown ink, brown and some blue wash, over preliminary indications in black chalk, a few corrections in white body color. The drawing consists of six sheets originally pinned together; that executed in black chalk only lacks the upper right corner. The whole measures about 24 x 22⅝ inches (about 610 x 570 mm.). Two sheets are signed by the artist in pen and ink: *B. West 1819*; a third is inscribed along the lower margin in pen and ink by another hand: *The last design by Benjⁿ West – | 1819–*. Watermark on each of the six sheets: . . . iping 1813 and Britannia.

If the inscriptions on this drawing and No. 1 are to be believed, the Morgan Library has the distinction of owning Benjamin West's first and last compositional sketches, which span a career of more than sixty years. The present drawing, evidently a preparatory design for a large painting, which probably was never executed due to the artist's death in March 1820, is closely related to the Boston drawing *Christ in the Hall of Caiphas* (Fig. 37); it is, in fact, a variant composition of the scene on the right in the Boston drawing where Peter is seen denying Christ as the maid recognizes him as one of Christ's disciples and where the crowing cock appears above them under the arch at right. Since Christ undoubtedly was to be the focal point of the action, one should perhaps postulate the existence of additional drawings making up the left half of the composition.

All the characteristics of West's drawings from the late period are present: the mere outlining of the figures, their bland facial expressions, and the summary treatment of anatomical detail and draperies. West had painted the same subject for King George III in about 1778 and once again for the chapel of Lord Newark (see *Supplement to La Belle Assemblée* of 1808, p. 15). The former which is now at St. James's Palace, London (see Millar, *op. cit.*, no. 1150, pl. 117), shows only the three principal figures in contrast to the many-figured cartoon-like scheme of the Library's drawing.

There is a preparatory drawing for the figure of Christ initialed by the artist at the Historical Society of Pennsylvania, Philadelphia (Vol. II of original drawings, p. 7; pen and brown ink, brown wash, 11¾ x 7⅞ inches).

108

Head of an Apostle
1970.11:182   PLATE 69

Black chalk. 12¾ x 9½ inches (322 x 241 mm.). Loss in upper right corner. Watermark: Turkey Mill / J. Whatman 1818.

This fine head of a bearded old man, perhaps the apostle St. Peter, may have been drawn by West in preparation for the figure of the disciple in *Christ in the Hall of Caiphas* (Fig. 37) or *Peter's Denial of Christ* (No. 107); in its nobility, it recalls St. Peter in the earlier version of the subject, now at St. James's Palace, London (see Millar, *op. cit.*, no. 1150, pl. 117). The delicate modeling of the face as well as the careful delineation of hair and beard make it an unusual example of West's draughtsmanship in these last years of his life.

109

Stag Hunt

1970.11:241 PLATE 104

Black chalk on light brown paper. 7¹¹⁄₁₆ x 7⁷⁄₁₆ inches
(195 x 188 mm.). Watermark: None.

This sketch can perhaps be connected with the
drawing of a hunting scene at the British Museum
(Book of Drawings, 198 b 10, p. 20; pen, brown
ink and brown wash on light brown paper, 5¹⁄₁₆ x 8
inches) which shows a stag being released from the
open doors of a wagon or cart and several hunters
on horseback. Both sketches were apparently made
from nature, perhaps on the occasion of one of the
royal hunts. The frenzy of the pack of howling
hounds and the anguish of the beast they are at-
tacking have been realistically rendered by the
artist. A rider who is driving on the dogs is visible
at the upper left.

The drawing can perhaps be related to "the
small picture of the death of the Stag" and a
drawing of the same subject mentioned in the *Supplement to La Belle Assemblée* on page 19 and also by
Galt (*Life*, II, p. 234).

110

Nude Figure Comforted by an Angel

1970.11:222

Pen and brown ink. 2¹⁄₁₆ x 3³⁄₈ inches (53 x 85 mm.).
Laid down.

Were the nude figure more clearly that of a youth,
this small pen sketch might be thought to represent Ishmael in the desert saved from death by an
angel bringing him water; the summary indication
of an overturned vase in the lower left corner
would suggest this interpretation. West evidently
decided to reduce the height of the composition
when he drew the horizontal line across his design.

111

Scene from ''The Golden Ass'' (?)

1970.11:189

Pen and gray ink. 3¹¹⁄₁₆ x 3¹³⁄₁₆ inches (94 x 96 mm.).

Laid down. Signed in black chalk by the artist at
lower right: *B. West.*

As the presence of an ass at the upper right would
suggest, this small compositional sketch may represent an episode from Lucius Apuleius' *Metamorphoses*, better known as *The Golden Ass.* The most
famous story incorporated in Apuleius' novel is the
tale of Cupid and Psyche, and the scene of the
Morgan drawing may well be taken from this part
of the book. West devoted at least two paintings to
the popular neo-classical subject of Cupid and
Psyche: *The Eagle Bringing the Cup of Water to
Psyche*, now at the Art Museum, Princeton University, Princeton, New Jersey (dated c. 1805 in the
catalogue of the 1938 West exhibition at the Pennsylvania Museum of Art, Philadelphia [n. 57]),
and the *Cupid and Psyche* of 1808 at the Corcoran
Gallery, Washington, D.C.

112

Female Deity Presenting a Woman to a Man

1970.11:47

Pen and brown ink. 3½ x 2½ inches (90 x 63 mm.).
Laid down. Initialed by the artist in black chalk at
lower left: *B W.*

The relationship of these figures is reminiscent of
representations of the creation of Eve but the presence of the full-length, robed woman suggests a
mythological subject like Pandora and Epimetheus, although Pandora is usually introduced to
Epimetheus by Mercury instead of the female
deity (Venus?) seen here.

FIGURES

113

*Study of a Male Nude, Three-Quarter-
Length*

1970.11:98 PLATES 70 AND 71

Black chalk, heightened with white, on gray-brown
paper. 12⁷⁄₈ x 9⁵⁄₈ inches (326 x 245 mm.). Losses at
upper right and lower right corners. Initialed by the
artist in pen and brown ink at lower left: *B. W–.* Verso:
Study of same nude, full-length but without head, in
black chalk. Watermark: None.

This study of a male nude, perhaps an athlete, is reminiscent of the figure of Hercules in West's painting *The Choice of Hercules*, signed and dated 1764, at the Victoria & Albert Museum, London. The facial type and the curly hair as well as the proportions of the body are similar. G. Evans (*West*, pp. 41–42, 47, pls. 20–21) has pointed out the similarity in type and pose of the figure of Hercules in the painting to the Vatican Meleager, and the Morgan Library's drawing also may reflect some ancient sculpture, perhaps Zeus hurling thunderbolts, which the artist could have seen in Rome in 1760–63.

114

Two Sketches of a Male Nude Seated on a Rock, and Study of Arm
1970.11:195

Black chalk, heightened with white, on gray-brown paper. 6¹⁵⁄₁₆ x 10⁵⁄₁₆ inches (176 x 262 mm.). Watermark on the old mat which has been removed: Letters IHS surmounted by cross (fragment; close to Heawood 2969–70).

These sketches of a sinewy bearded athlete possibly represent Hercules, as the club on which one of the figures leans suggests. On the left Hercules seems to be resting from his labors as the man on the right rubs down with a cloth. Both figures, in type and pose, are vaguely reminiscent of the bronze figure of a boxer at the Museo Nazionale Romano or a similar statue. These early sketches attest to the strong impression ancient sculpture left with the young artist during his student days in Italy. Galt tells of the excitement the Apollo Belvedere aroused in West who exclaimed: "My God, how like it is to a young Mohawk warrior!" A drawing by West of the Apollo is preserved at the Friends Historical Library, Swarthmore College (29, C-7; black chalk on brown paper, 11¹⁵⁄₁₆ x 8¾ inches).

115

Male Nude Seated on a Rock
1970.11:102   PLATE 72

Pen and brown ink, pink and blue watercolor. 24⅝ x 17⅞ inches (625 x 454 mm.). Laid down. Signed and dated in pen and brown ink at left center: *B. West 1783*.

This carefully executed academic study of a seated male nude dates from one of the most prolific and artistically successful periods of West's career. Most of the drawings made in the 1780's are fine examples of draughtsmanship, and the addition of watercolor gives these sheets special appeal. The drawing *Jacob and Laban* in the Print Room of the New York Public Library is another typical example.

The precise rendering of every detail in the present drawing (for example, the hair), the fine hatchings used in modeling the various parts of the body, and the strong outlines giving the figure an almost sculptural appearance all suggest that West may have used a drawing like this in his capacity as teacher of design at the Royal Academy. In his discourse to the students of this institution in 1794, on the occasion of the distribution of prizes (Galt, *op. cit.*, II, pp. 93–102), he stressed the importance of mastering the human figure and cited the Apollo Belvedere and the Venus de' Medici as the perfect models. It is interesting to note that there is in the British Museum an *Academical Study for an Eve*,

Fig. 39 LEWIS SCHIAVONETTI.
"Academical Study for an Eve." Engraving. *London, British Museum.*

a proof impression of an engraving by Lewis Schiavonetti after an original drawing signed and dated *B. West 1784* (38-7-14-72; 24⅝ x 17½ inches. Fig. 39), which was included in G. Minasi's *Academical Studies after great Masters* published in London in 1814.

The figure of Eve in the print, it may be remarked, carries reminiscences of the Medici Venus. Since the Morgan Library's drawing is almost identical in size and signed with similar flourish, it may have been intended for the same publication.

116

Study of Two Toes
1970.11:162

Pen and brown ink on light brown paper. 3⅞ x 4⅞ inches (87 x 112 mm.).

This study of two toes, possibly a detail of the foot of the nude man in the drawing 1970.11:102 (No. 115), can perhaps also be related to West's teaching activity at the Royal Academy. The toes, however, have not been drawn in the same foreshortened view as in the large drawing and may have been copied from a statue or plaster cast.

117

Male Nude Subduing a Serpent
1970.11:22   PLATE 73

Black chalk, heightened with white, on light brown paper. 24⅝ x 17¾ inches (617 x 450 mm.). Water stain at lower left corner. The name *B. West*, which was inscribed in pen and brown ink at lower left, has been rubbed out. Watermark: None.

This unusually large sheet and the following drawing, both of which are almost equal in size with the preceding study, may likewise have been connected with West's teaching activity at the Royal Academy despite the fact that the present drawing and the *Standing Male Nude* (No. 118), though probably drawn after the model, are not academic studies in the strict sense. The nude man placing one foot on a huge serpent holds a club in his right hand and grasps its tail with the left. The figure with its enigmatic expression and strangely agitated hair lends itself to various interpretations.

Fig. 40   Samson Bound.
London, British Museum.

One thinks of Satan or Cadmus slaying the serpent. The modeling of the muscular body is very similar to *Samson Bound*, a drawing in the British Museum which is signed and dated *B. West 1788 Windsor* (1887-16-13-0; brush and watercolor, heightened with white body color, 20⅝ x 11¾ inches. Fig. 40). It is barely possible that Laocoön, the central figure of the famous Hellenistic sculpture, is vaguely reflected in the stance of this figure who is also wrestling with a serpent.

118

Standing Male Nude
1970.11:101   PLATE 74

Black chalk. 25 x 17¾ inches (635 x 450 mm.). Several

Fig. 41   Moses Receiving the Laws on Mount Sinai.
London, Palace of Westminster.

tears along upper margin; water stain in lower left corner. Watermark: Pieter van der Ley (similar to lower part of Churchill 113).

The male nude holding a knife or dagger in his raised hand and leaning on a large book with his left, in type as well as pose, somewhat resembles the figure of Moses in *Moses Receiving the Laws on Mount Sinai* of 1784, originally executed for the King's Chapel, Windsor, and now in the Palace of Westminster near St. Stephen's entrance (canvas, 19 x 13 inches. Fig. 41).

119

Sketches of the Parthenon Metopes (*Elgin Marbles*)

1970.11:135   PLATE 76

Black chalk. 7⅜ x 4⅜ inches (182 x 111 mm.). Irregular left margin. Verso: Black chalk sketches of Abraham and Isaac (?). Watermark: [Turke]y Mill [1]806.

The greater part of the Elgin marbles had arrived safely from Greece by January 1804. In the summer of 1807 they were installed in a shed on the grounds of Lord Elgin's house at the corner of Park Lane and Piccadilly, London, and permission was given to selected visitors to view the sculptures there; among those admitted was Benjamin West. He was deeply affected by the Elgin marbles. Farington quotes him in his diary entry of 30 March 1808: "He [West] sd. that they were sublime specimens of the purest sculpture, & that when the summer arrives He means to devote much time to study from them. He sd. that this He wd. do though in His 70th year, & had on this acct. a wish to be again only 20 years of age & that He might labour to profit by them. . . ."

These sketches were made by West from the Elgin marbles, now in the British Museum. On this sheet, he was studying the Battle of the Centaurs and the Lapiths (see D. E. L. Haynes, *An Historical Guide to the Sculptures of the Parthenon*, 1971, figs. 21 and 20). The prostrate figure at the top is copied directly from South Metope XXVIII, but the center and bottom sketches are "paraphrases" of the reliefs, undeniably, however, inspired by them. For instance, the left half of the drawing at the bottom is taken from South Metope XXVII.

Following the display at Lord Elgin's residence, the marbles were transferred to Burlington House and in January 1817 they found a permanent home in the British Museum. (A view of the gallery in which they were first shown to the public appears in a painting by A. Archer; Benjamin West is seen seated in the foreground; see Haynes, *op. cit.*, illus. opp. title page.)

The two verso sketches of a figure, rushing out of the clouds toward a man with upraised right arm, evidently trying to stop him from whatever he is about to do, can perhaps be interpreted as the Angel of the Lord restraining Abraham from sacrificing his son, in accordance with the text of Genesis XXII.

120

Seated Male Nude

1970.11:168   PLATE 77

Black chalk, heightened with white, on blue-gray

paper. 7⁹⁄₁₆ x 11⅞ inches (193 x 302 mm.). Stain along right margin. Watermark: None.

This and the following academic study of a seated youth were perhaps executed by West in the course of his teaching activity at the Royal Academy. But the present drawing may also reflect the inspiration West received from the study of the Elgin marbles (see No. 119). There is a certain similarity in the pose with that of the so-called Theseus or Heracles (?) from the east pediment of the Parthenon (Haynes, *op. cit.*, fig. 24).

121

Seated Male Nude with a Cup
1970.11:167

Black chalk, heightened with white, on blue-gray paper. 11⅛ x 8⅛ inches (282 x 206 mm.). Verso: Landscape and other sketches in black chalk. Watermark: None.

122

Seated Man and Torso
1970.11:184   PLATE 75

Black chalk, heightened with white, on light brown paper. 17³⁄₁₆ x 11⁹⁄₁₆ inches (438 x 294 mm.). Verso: Black chalk sketch of leg. Watermark: None.

The pose of the seated nude is similar to that of the figure in the preceding drawing. Obviously unfinished, this drawing may have been made by West with a figure in a painting in mind as there is more emphasis on the modeling of the body and the contrast between light and shaded areas than in the two preceding drawings where the stress on the clean outlines of the forms of the youthful, athletic bodies is more in keeping with their purpose as academic studies.

123

Male Nude Seen from the Back
1970.11:133

Black chalk. 9½ x 9⅞ inches (249 x 250 mm.). Watermark: Fleur-de-lis.

124

Female Nude with Windblown Hair
1970.11:255

Black chalk. 6½ x 4⁹⁄₁₆ inches (165 x 116 mm.). Watermark: J. Wh[atman].

Like the preceding drawing, this sketch of a female nude may have been made with a mythological figure in mind, perhaps Venus in *Venus Rising from the Sea* (H. Moses, *op. cit.*, pl. 2).

125

Prostrate Female Nude
1970.11:96

Black chalk. 3⅜ x 5⅝ inches (85 x 143 mm.). Framed with gray wash on old mat. Watermark: None.

The lightly sketched nude—some *pentimenti* are noticeable in the lower part of the body—bears a strong resemblance to the prostrate woman of the family group in *Death on a Pale Horse* (Fig. 20).

126

Two Sketches of a Female Nude with Long Hair
1970.11:229

Pen and brown ink. 5⁷⁄₁₆ x 4⁵⁄₁₆ inches (138 x 111 mm.). Inscribed in pen and brown ink on verso: *Benjamin West Esq!* | & & | *at Windsor.* Postal stamp dated OC[tober] 17/94.

Since the woman on the left seems to be chained, she can perhaps be presumed to represent Andromeda or St. Margaret; the swirling clouds and the foliage at upper right indicate a landscape setting.

127

Studies of Hands
1970.11:105   PLATE 78

Black chalk, heightened with white, on oatmeal paper. 21 x 12⅝ inches (530 x 322 mm.). Stains along upper margin. Verso: Black chalk studies of two hands. Watermark: None.

Although it has not been possible to connect these hands with any particular composition in West's *oeuvre,* they can be found with slight variations in many of his paintings; for instance, the hands on the recto of this sheet resemble those of the angel in the painting of the *Resurrection* of 1782 (Fig. 16), where there is also the gnarled, expressive hand of an apostle with lean and bony fingers, very similar to one of the hands on the verso of this sheet reproduced here.

128

Study of a Woman's Hand
1970.11:83   PLATE 79

Black chalk, heightened with white, on blue paper. 10 x 5¾ inches (253 x 146 mm.). Watermark: None.

This and the following study of a hand are fine drawings, perhaps dating from the years 1770–80. The slim, feminine right hand in this sketch with its long, tapering fingers may be compared with Una's left hand in the painting *Una and the Lion* of 1772 at the Wadsworth Atheneum, Hartford, Connecticut (Evans, *West,* pl. 30). The black chalk used for the outlines and shadows and the white highlights are combined in a pleasing effect in this study.

129

Study of a Hand
1970.11:172

Black chalk, heightened with white, on blue paper. 5⅝ x 3¾ inches (111 x 96 mm.). Verso: Fragments of two compositional sketches. Watermark: None.

The small broad hand with foreshortened fingers, perhaps that of a boy, can be found in some of West's paintings executed in the decade 1770–80; compare, for instance, Ishmael's hand in the Metropolitan Museum's painting *Hagar and Ishmael* of 1776, retouched 1803 (Evans, *West,* pl. 38).

130

Ecorché Leg
1970.11:99

Black chalk, heightened with white, on blue paper. 10⅟₁₆ x 5¹¹⁄₁₆ inches (256 x 145 mm.). Verso: Fragment of compositional sketch (perhaps for a Nativity or an Adoration). Watermark: None.

This careful delineation of the intricate interweaving of the muscles and tendons in the human leg may be connected with West's role as instructor at the Royal Academy. In all his discourses to the students of this institution he emphasized the importance of the study of the human figure. "In your progress through that mechanical part of your professional education, which is directed to the acquisition of a perfect knowledge of the human figure, I recommend to you a scrupulous exactness in imitating what is immediately before you . . ." (Galt, *Life,* II, pp. 108–09). Further on in the same speech, he enumerates in great detail the parts of the body, which should be "taken in three points of view, the front, back, and profile," including besides head, neck, thorax, etc., also "thigh, knee, leg, ankle, the carpus, metacarpus, and toes" (see No. 78).

The sketch of a seated woman in an architectural setting on the verso of this sheet was perhaps made for a figure of the Virgin in connection with a Nativity or an Adoration of the Magi.

131

The Death of Cleopatra
1970.11:234

Black chalk, some stumping. Diameter: 6⅝ inches (160 mm.). Laid down. Inscribed in graphite by another hand on old mount at lower right: *B. West / Study from life for the death of Cleopatra;* at lower left: *£2.2–.*

This circular drawing, which has been cut out and laid down on a rectangular sheet of heavy paper, must have been included in a sale of West drawings held not too long after the artist's death. Although the inscription, which was perhaps added at the time of the sale, refers to a composition of the death of Cleopatra, no painting of this subject is recorded. West may have used the same model for Procris in *Cephalus Lamenting the Death of Procris*, dated 1770, the painting at the Art Institute of Chicago.

132

Sheet of Sketches
1970.11:225

Pen and gray ink. 11¼ x 8⅛ inches (285 x 205 mm.). Watermark: None.

This sheet of rough sketches includes a variety of motives: a large male head in three-quarter view, part of a bent over nude figure, a man in a wide-brimmed hat, and a seated female nude, her head inclined on her shoulder. The latter figure seems to be either dying or asleep, her pose recalling that of the figure of Adonis in *Venus Lamenting the Death of Adonis* of 1772 at the Carnegie Institute, Pittsburgh, Pennsylvania (Evans, *West*, pl. 31).

133

Young Man in a Leopard Skin and Phrygian Headdress
1970.11:136

Black chalk. 7⅜ x 4½ inches (187 x 114 mm.). Watermark: Horn with letters G R (close to Heawood 1753 and 1756).

134

Seated Figure in a Turban
1970.11:260

Black chalk. 4¹⁵⁄₁₆ x 6⅛ inches (125 x 155 mm.). Stain.

The oriental costume suggests that the figure can perhaps be related to *An Embassy in the East*, a drawing signed and dated *B. West 1774*, at the British Museum (1895.2.25.1; pen and brown ink, brown wash, 4⅝ x 7⅝ inches).

135

Seated Woman with Headdress
1970.11:74

Black chalk. 3⁵⁄₁₆ x 2³⁄₁₆ inches (85 x 55 mm.). Laid down.

This young woman seated in profile view, one hand resting on her lap, the other supporting her chin, wears a costume similar to that of the young mother in the painting *The Golden Age* of 1776 at the Tate Gallery, and a mood of quiet contemplation prevails in both the painting and the drawing. One cannot, however, point to any specific connection between them. The stitching along the left margin suggests that the sheet is a sketchbook leaf.

136

Two Putti
1970.11:78

Black chalk. 3³⁄₁₆ x 2¾ inches (82 x 70 mm.). Signed in black chalk by the artist at lower left: *B. West.* Upper part of a letter inscribed in pen and brown ink at lower right. Watermark: None.

These two curly-haired cherubs, who seem to be sketched from life, have their peers in the groups of small angels accompanying the principal figure in such book illustrations as the frontispiece to Volume XII of the *New English Theatre* of 1777 (Fig. 5).

137

Fisherman in a Large Hat
1970.11:231

Black chalk. 4¹³⁄₁₆ x 4¹⁄₁₆ inches (122 x 103 mm.). Watermark: None.

The fisherman seated on a rock and holding a fishing rod is vaguely reminiscent of one of Salvator Rosa's figures in a drawing at the Royal Library, Windsor Castle (see E. Schilling, *The German Drawings . . . and Supplements to the Catalogues of Italian and French Drawings*, London and New York, 1973, no. 404, pl. 44). Such a drawing by Rosa or perhaps a print may have inspired West who is known to have admired the Italian artist and owned several prints by J. Goupy after landscapes by Rosa and possibly some drawings as well.

138

Seated Woman Seen from the Back
1970.11:170

Black chalk, heightened with white, on blue-gray paper. 11³⁄₁₆ x 7¹³⁄₁₆ inches (284 x 198 mm.). Verso: Outline of head in black chalk. Watermark: None.

This rapid sketch of a seated woman which effectively catches the movement of the body and the turn of the head has not as yet been identified with any particular painting. West liked to place figures with their backs to the spectator in the foreground of his compositions as a means of rounding out these compositions or as *repoussoirs* intended to guide the viewer's eye into the picture toward the action. The Morgan figure may be compared to the woman at the lower left of West's painting of *The Raising of Lazarus* of 1780 at the Wadsworth Atheneum, Hartford, Connecticut (Evans, *West*, pl. 8).

139

Sketch of a Female Demon
1970.11:239

Pen and brown ink, brown wash. 6³⁄₈ x 8³⁄₁₆ inches (161 x 208 mm.). Watermark: Royal ciphers and crown within circle (close to Churchill 248).

It is surprising to find a finished sketch of a grotesque creature like this bat-like demon among the Library's West drawings. The bony face with its bulging eyes, and the scrawny limbs and dugs make this demon a companion of the fantastic creatures in the train of Death in the several versions of *Death on a Pale Horse* (Fig. 20).

140

"The Fashion of 1782"
1970.11:257

Pen and brown ink. 4⅝ x 4 inches (117 x 102 mm.).

Lower corners slightly cropped. Inscribed in pen and ink at upper right, presumably by the artist: *Fashion of 1782*. Watermark: None.

Could this elegantly attired young gentleman wearing a bag-wig possibly be West's son Raphael, who would have been sixteen years old in 1782? He had been a handsome child, and Mrs. Papendiek, the Queen's Mistress of the Wardrobe, mentions him in her memoirs as a natty dresser (see Helmut von Erffa, "Benjamin West at the Height of His Career," *The American Art Journal*, 1, Spring 1969, p. 26 and footnote 24). She speaks as well of "large cravats and curly hair, and other extravagant fashion, set by the Prince of Wales."

141

Head of a Young Woman
1970.11:97   PLATE 80

Black chalk. 9 x 6⅞ inches (228 x 164 mm.). Stain at upper left. Watermark: Fragment of horn (Heawood 2742).

The profile of a young woman may have been drawn from life. This seems to be borne out by a comparison with the lovely drawing of a *Mother and Child*, signed and dated *B. West 1783* at the Boston Museum of Fine Arts (Acc. No. 42.595; pen and brown wash, touched with light blue watercolor, 7 x 4¹³⁄₁₆ inches), which is inscribed in pen and brown ink on the back of the old mount: *A Mother and Child. Study from Nature. Benjⁿ. West*. There the same woman, or certainly a very similar type, displays the same regular features, her hair falling over her shoulders and her gaze directed downward; she wears, however, a turban-like headdress of sheer material.

142

Standing Man Holding His Hat
1970.11:70

Pen and black ink. 4¹³⁄₁₆ x 7 inches (121 x 179 mm.). Verso: Black chalk sketch of a multi-figured composition. Watermark: None.

This sketch was probably made from life.

143

Half-Length Figure of a Man with Folded Arms

1970.11:38

Black chalk on blue paper. 10 1/16 x 7 1/16 inches (255 x 180 mm.). Watermark: None.

This strong drawing of a burly man, his arms folded across his chest, is an early work. West represented two of the figures in the earlier version of *St. Peter Denying Christ*, St. James's Palace, London, in a similar pose (see Millar, *op. cit.*, no. 1150, pl. 117). The sturdily built, bare-chested sailor type also occurs in some of West's multi-figured compositions, for instance, *St. Paul Shaking Off the Viper* at the Tate Gallery, London, and *The Conversion of St. Paul* of 1786 at the Smith College Museum of Art, Northampton, Massachusetts.

144

Sailor

1970.11:55 PLATE 82

Black chalk. 10 1/2 x 7 5/8 inches (267 x 193 mm.). Watermark: Coat-of-arms with fleur-de-lis surmounted by crown (close to Churchill 416).

The sailor nonchalantly leaning on his sabre wears the same costume as the seaman represented on a recent British 7 1/2 pence commemorative postage stamp inscribed *H M Coastguard 1822/1972*: a blue jacket, over a white waistcoat, white trousers, a black kerchief tied loosely around the neck, and a round hat with turned up brim. West may have seen a type like this at Margate or another seaport near London. Such a sketch can perhaps be associated with the drawing *Characters in the Streets of London*, signed and dated *B. West 1799*, formerly at the Berry-Hill Galleries, New York.

145

Man in Classical Tunic Gesticulating, a Seated Nude Woman at His Feet

1970.11:49

Pen and brown ink, on gray paper. 4 3/4 x 7 1/16 inches (122 x 179 mm.). Verso: Sketch of similar group. Watermark: None.

What theme West was illustrating in the rough compositional sketches on both sides of this sheet remains to be identified. In both sketches the male figure, attired in a classical tunic on the recto sketch and a beret and cloak on the verso, is seen pointing out something in the distance to a seated woman or perhaps dismissing her with a dramatic gesture. Were there a child present, one might think of the subject of Abraham casting out Hagar and Ishmael.

146

Man in an Attitude of Fear

1970.11:198

Black chalk. 7 5/16 x 4 5/8 inches (186 x 117 mm.). Irregular left margin. Red seals, one on recto, the other on verso. Inscribed on verso in pen and brown ink: *Benamin West Esqr / Newman Street.* Watermark: None.

This rough sketch of a giant apparently stalking a frightened man has so far eluded any attempt to connect it with a known composition. The towering figure, if he actually swings a censer as he appears to do, might be interpreted as Aaron staying the plague (see No. 52).

147

Half-Length Figure in State of Fright

1970.11:263

Black chalk on gray paper. 6 3/4 x 5 7/8 inches (171 x 149 mm.). Watermark: None.

The Medusa-like head with its tousled hair and expression of terror is a pure example of West's so-called dread manner. It may be compared with the face of Achilles in *Thetis Bringing the Armor to Achilles* of 1806 at the New Britain Museum of American Art, New Britain, Connecticut.

148

Soldier with Plumed Shako

1970.11:34 PLATE 81

Black chalk on blue paper. 12 1/8 x 5 13/16 inches (308 x

148 mm.). Verso: Black chalk sketch of three doves.

The soldier's uniform in this drawing can perhaps be identified as that of a Royal Fusilier (see A. E. Haswell Miller and N. P. Dawnay, *Military Drawings and Paintings in the Collection of Her Majesty the Queen*, London, 1966, I, pl. 477, third figure from left). The shako especially is similar to that worn by soldiers at the battle of Waterloo in 1815 (*op. cit.*, no. 2479). Two of the doves on the verso appear in West's painting *Omnia Vincit Amor* of 1811 at the Metropolitan Museum of Art (Evans, *West*, pl. 60). There they are held by Venus, whose hand is just faintly visible in the drawing. For another of West's sketches of birds, see *Pigeons Feeding* in the British Museum (1887.6.13.7; black chalk on blue paper, 3¼ x 4½ inches), evidently drawn from nature.

149

Man in Highland Dress
1970.11:80   PLATE 82

Oval design. Pen and brown ink over preliminary drawing in graphite; dog sketched in black chalk. 8¼ x 7⅟₁₆ inches (210 x 180 mm.). Inscribed in pen and brown ink at lower right on the plough: *1817 | B. West*. Notations in graphite on right of design by a different hand: *Shield on arm | Plaid over belt | feather on left side | the slow hound | Purse*. Watermark: Ivy Mill | 1805.

The Scot, in his kilt, holding a sword in his right hand and the handle of a plough in his left, may somehow be connected with the engraved membership form of the Highland Society in London, of which there is an example at the British Museum (1859.7.9.1581; 23⅛ x 16⅞ inches. Fig. 42), inscribed *B. West, Esq. P.R.A. Pinxᵗ., L. Clennell, Sculpᵗ*. (The Highland Society, according to the inscription on the form, was instituted in May 1778.)

150

Running Soldier with Helmet and Shield
1970.11:152

Pen and black ink on gray paper. 12⅜ x 15½ inches (310 x 394 mm.). Some pen trials along upper margin. Watermark: None.

The figure has been drawn on the back of an old mount from which another drawing was detached.

Fig. 42   LUKE CLENNELL.
Membership Form of Highland Society, London.
Engraving.
London, British Museum.

151

Half-Length Reclining Figure
1970.11:143

Pen and brown ink on gray paper. 5¾ x 5⁹⁄₁₆ inches (146 x 141 mm.). Watermark: None.

PORTRAITS

152

Family Group in Front of a House
1970.11:183   PLATE 83

Black chalk on gray paper. 7⅞ x 7 inches (200 x 178 mm.). Brown stain at upper left. Verso: Two sketches of boys, one on horseback; a landscape. Watermark: None.

This might possibly be the West family in front of their house. If so, the woman holding a baby, perhaps Benjamin West, Jr., is Mrs. West, and the two older boys may be Raphael and a playmate. An older woman, perhaps a servant, is standing in the doorway. A big dog and a small one appear at lower left. The rustic atmosphere suggests that the house is located in the country, and it is known from West's letter of 25 July 1769, addressed to Dr. Jonathan Morris, that in addition to his house in London where he carried on his profession, he maintained a house in the country "four miles distant from Town." His "little Family" consisted at that time of his wife, Raphael, and a servant or two (see *The Pennsylvania Magazine of History and Biography*, XVIII, no. 1, 1894, pp. 219–20). Assuming that the baby on the woman's arm is Benjamin West, Jr. (born 1772), who appears to be about a year old, a date of about 1773 would be established for the drawing. It brings to mind the small sketch of a woman holding a baby signed *B. West* in the collection of Mr. and Mrs. Paul Mellon (pencil, 4 x 3 inches). The little boy and a pony on the verso of the Morgan drawing would be seven-year-old Raphael.

153

Portrait Head of a Lady
1970.11:120   PLATE 84

Black chalk. 14⅜ x 10½ inches (365 x 268 mm.). Stains throughout; horizontal crease at center. Watermark: Britannia with letters IWS and crown with letters GR (Heawood 221, c. 1789).

The attractive sitter may perhaps be Queen Charlotte, wife of King George III (1744–1818). Comparing her features as delineated in this drawing with those in West's formal full-length painted portrait of the Queen at Windsor Castle, signed and dated 1779 (Millar, *op. cit.*, no. 1139, pl. 109), one detects a certain resemblance in the oval contour of the face, the high forehead, the straight nose, the pretty well-formed mouth, and the almond-shaped eyes. The similarity of features is even stronger with those of Thomas Gainsborough's half-length portrait of Queen Charlotte of 1782 at Windsor Castle (Millar, *op. cit.*, no. 779, pl. 50), which shows the Queen wearing a triangular lace

cap and *fichu*, just as in the drawing. Queen Charlotte was thirty-eight years old when Gainsborough painted the 1782 portrait.

154

Head of a Boy (*Prince Octavius?*)
1970.11:73   PLATE 80

Graphite. 4⁷⁄₁₆ x 4⅞ inches (112 x 124 mm.). Two vertical creases. Watermark: None.

One cannot but sense a certain portrait quality in this profile of a curly-headed small boy, and it is tempting to identify him with Prince Octavius, one of the two sons of King George III who died in infancy and were immortalized in West's painting *The Apotheosis of Prince Octavius*, 1783, now at Buckingham Palace (see Oliver Millar, *op. cit.*, no. 1149, pl. 116). The resemblance seems to be even stronger in the two preparatory drawings for this painting: one in the Boston Museum of Fine Arts showing studies for the principal figures in the painting (Acc. No. 42.607; pen and brown ink, brown wash, on cream paper, 17⁷⁄₁₆ x 11¹⁵⁄₁₆ inches); the other, a compositional drawing in the Sir Robert Witt Collection, Courtauld Institute of Art, London (615; pen and sepia and color wash, 7½ x 8¾ inches; see Oliver Millar, *op. cit.*, figs. 38 and 39). A comparison with the full-length portrait of the prince holding the King's sword at Windsor Castle, another of West's paintings of 1783 (see Oliver Millar, *op. cit.*, no. 1148, pl. 113), although representing the boy in frontal view, also suggests that the subject in the Morgan Library's sketch may be the young prince who died on 3 May 1783 at the age of four.

155

Portrait of an Elderly Man with Long Hair
1970.11:11   PLATE 85

Pen and brown ink. 4¹³⁄₁₆ x 7 inches (122 x 179 mm.). Signed in pen and brown ink at lower right: *B. West. Windsor. 1784*. Verso: Black chalk and gray wash drawing of a landscape with gnarled tree trunks. Watermark: None.

This likeness of an elderly man with long hair, seen

in profile view, shows West's deftness in rendering the individuality of a subject with a few swift strokes of the pen. Unfortunately, the identity of the sitter cannot be readily determined. One can perhaps rule out the artist's father, John West, who died in 1776. It might, however, be a portrait of West's half brother, Thomas, whom the elder West had left behind in England when he emigrated to America in 1714; Thomas must have been in his seventies in 1784. At any rate, the portrait and the landscape on the verso are fine examples of West's most successful period as a draughtsman.

156

Hand in a Sleeve Holding Open Book
Study for the Portrait of Mrs. Peter Beckford (Bathshua Hering Beckford), Metropolitan Museum of Art, New York.

1970.11:165   PLATE 88

Black chalk, heightened with white, on blue-gray paper. 5¹⁵⁄₁₆ x 8⁹⁄₁₆ inches (151 x 217 mm.). Watermark: None.

The Metropolitan Museum's portraits of Mr. and Mrs. Peter Beckford, the parents of Alderman William Beckford and the grandparents of William Beckford, the author of *Vathek*, are signed and dated *B. West 1797*. Since Peter Beckford died in 1735 and his wife about 1750, their likenesses were evidently based on earlier portraits. The seventeenth-century costume worn by the sitters lends support to this assumption. These two portraits as well as those of Mrs. William Beckford (see No. 158) and the Countess of Effingham at the National Gallery of Art, Washington, D.C., were commissioned by William Beckford and hung at Fonthill Abbey. Their larger than life scale suggests that Beckford intended these ancestral portraits for the decoration of the medieval halls of Fonthill Abbey above the many coats-of-arms and heraldic devices attesting to his noble birth. There is a preparatory drawing for the portrait of Mrs. Peter Beckford at the Friends Historical Library, Swarthmore College (P.P.246); it is also executed in black chalk, heightened with white, on blue paper (10¹³⁄₁₆ x 8¹⁵⁄₁₆ inches).

This and the following drawing, which is executed in the same medium, show West's accomplished draughtsmanship in this period of his career. The successful rendering of forms and textiles and the effective use of highlights give them their special attraction.

157

Drapery Study
1970.11:100

Black chalk, heightened with white, on blue-gray paper. 15⅛ x 9¾ inches (382 x 249 mm.). Watermark: IV.

This drawing may be connected with Mrs. Peter Beckford's portrait or a similar picture. Executed in the same medium as the *Study of a Hand in a Sleeve* (No. 156), it shows a heavy drapery with an embroidered border and fringed edge which West liked to use as a decorative backdrop in many of his portraits. The curved lines along the lower margin seem to indicate the back of the sitter's chair and the vertical line at right, the edge of the composition.

158

Seated Woman with a Musical Instrument
Study for the Portrait of Mrs. William Beckford (1724/5–98), National Gallery of Art, Washington, D. C. (Andrew Mellon Collection, 1947).

1970.11:188   PLATES 86 AND 87

Black chalk, heightened with white, on gray paper; some outlines reinforced with the pen and black ink. 10⁹⁄₁₆ x 8½ inches (269 x 216 mm.). Verso: Black chalk sketch for the same portrait. Watermark: Fleur-de-lis within circle.

The drawing shows a woman seated in the open air, her head turned to the right, holding an open book on her lap. The neck of a stringed musical instrument, perhaps a cello or viola da gamba, is visible at the right, a drapery and a bouquet of flowers at the left. There is a large house and wing with a colonnade in the background. This is Fonthill House, the old family mansion presumably built under the direction of James Paine in the period 1756–65; it preceded Fonthill Abbey, that grandiose and extremely costly neo-gothic structure begun on the initiative of the younger Beckford by the architect James Wyatt I in 1796. (The portico of a temple and a wooded hill with pheasants were added in the painting.) The sketch on the verso of the drawing shows the same figure seated in a similar pose; however, the bouquet of flowers is here on the right. Evidently the artist tried out various positions of the arms; for instance, in this sketch he considered the possibility of having the sitter arrange the flowers in a vase.

The catalogue of the National Gallery of Art, Washington, D.C. (*American Paintings and Sculpture*, Washington, 1970, p. 120), dates the painted portrait "probably 1799." It is one of a group of four family portraits which West painted for William Beckford, all about the same size and identically framed according to Mr. William P. Campbell, Curator, Department of American Paintings, The National Gallery of Art. Its companion is the portrait of Mrs. Beckford's sister-in-law, Elizabeth, Countess of Effingham (1725–91), also at the National Gallery; the other two portraits are those at the Metropolitan Museum of Art, New York, mentioned in No. 156.

William Beckford, Alderman and Mayor of London, married Maria, the eldest daughter of the Hon. George Hamilton, second son of the sixth Earl of Abercorn, and the widow of Francis Marsh, in 1756. Mrs. Beckford, whom her famous son referred to in his letters as "The Begum" and who is described by her son's biographers as a "matriarchal tyrant," died 22 July 1798, at the age of seventy-three or seventy-four. The Morgan Library's drawing as well as the painted portrait, however, shows a much younger person. Since West billed William Beckford for a portrait of his mother in September 1799 (statement interleaved in Galt, *Life*, folio ed., London, 1820, III, p. 69, at the Historical Society of Pennsylvania, Philadelphia), the Washington portrait of Mrs. Beckford—if indeed it is the portrait the above document refers to—must be based on an earlier portrait by West or perhaps on that by Andrea Casali made in 1768–69 as suggested by Boyd Alexander, Beckford's biographer. The sitter would then have been about forty-four years old. It is understandable that William Beckford wished these memorial portraits of his mother and of his aunt to show them as attractive mature women and not as dowagers of advanced age. The present drawing may have been made by Benjamin West in the summer of 1798 (see Farington Diary, I, p. 251) or in the following year when he was working on large religious paintings for Fonthill Abbey and the designs for its windows.

159

Half-Length Portrait of a Young Man in a Broad-Brimmed Hat
1970.11:176

Black chalk. 1¾ x 1½ inches (43 x 38 mm.). Laid down.

This tiny sketch of a young man seated at a table in front of a drapery background, resting his chin on his right hand, may be a self-portrait of the artist. He is similarly posed in several painted self-portraits, namely those in the National Gallery, Washington, D.C., and in the Blaustein collection. He appears in a similar broad-brimmed hat in *Landscape with Two Horsemen and Cattle Drinking* at the Victoria & Albert Museum, the painting which Ann C. Van Devanter ("Benjamin West and his Self-Portraits," *Antiques*, April 1973, p. 767, fig. 3) has identified as Lot 156 in George Robins' sale catalogue of 1829. There the artist, accompanied by his loyal servant James Dyer and their mounts, is seen leaning against a tree, sketchbook in hand. The painting is signed and dated *B. West 1799*.

160

Horseman with His Mount
1970.11:175

Brown and black chalk. 3¹⁵⁄₁₆ x 3³⁄₁₆ inches (100 x 81 mm.). Bordered in black chalk. Watermark: None.

This sketch of an elegant gentleman leaning nonchalantly against his horse may also, like the previous drawing, be a self-portrait. The subject wears a long coat and crosses his legs as in the Victoria & Albert Museum's painting *Landscape with Two Horsemen and Cattle Drinking* (see Ann C. Van Devanter, *op. cit.*, fig. 3). On the other hand, the sketch may represent a first idea for a portrait commission.

161

Three-Quarter-Length Portrait of Napoleon

1970.11:85   PLATE 89

Pen and brown ink. 3½ x 3 inches (90 x 76 mm.). Verso: Fragment of a letter or note in the artist's hand: *. . . which have distinguished | . . . assurance my profound respect | greatly obliged. | B.W.* Watermark: None.

This and the following drawing may have been made in connection with Benjamin West's trip to Paris in the fall of 1802 after the Peace of Amiens had been concluded in March of that year. He was one of the many artists—for instance, Fuseli, Flaxman, Farington, and Hoppner—who made the pilgrimage to Paris to see the art treasures—mostly trophies of war—assembled there. West was accompanied by his younger son and namesake; Raphael was still in America at that time. A sketchbook preserved at the Royal Academy in London contains sketches made while "travelling through France between Calais and Paris—1802—." According to Farington's diary entry of 24 September 1802, West was introduced to Napoleon in the Exhibition Room [the Salon at the Louvre] by the Minister of the Interior. When the Consul "came to His picture [*Death on a Pale Horse*, see No. 39] Bonaparte spoke to him in Italian, hoped he had found Paris agreeable and expressed his approbation of the merit of his picture." To ingratiate himself with his hosts in Paris and to reciprocate for their hospitality, West gave a "public breakfast, or rather dinner" on 27 September at his hotel to which he invited the most important French artists and museum officials (see Farington, *Diary*, II, pp. 33–34, for details, even to the seating arrangement). West was much impressed by Napoleon. Later on, in May 1815, when every Englishman saw in him the national enemy, Smirke is reported to have objected to West's and other persons' favorable comments about him and he remarked that "it was most extraordinary that men who professed themselves advocates of liberty should be so warped in their opinions" (Farington, *Diary*, VIII, p. 3).

Napoleon was a young man of thirty-three in 1802. West's sketch portrays him as First Consul (he had become Consul as of 24 December 1799). Intended perhaps as a preparatory sketch for a large portrait to be executed after his return to England, the Morgan sheet shows *pentimenti* in the position of the subject's right arm. The artist apparently first considered showing the Consul leaning on a table and then decided to represent him holding a letter or dispatch. A decorative drapery can be seen in the background at upper left.

162

Bonaparte's Carriage

1970.11:86   PLATE 89

Black chalk on gray paper. 5 x 6⅞ inches (126 x 164 mm.). Inscribed in graphite along lower margin: *Bounapartes Carriage – Drawn by*. Signed in graphite by the artist: *Benjⁿ West*. Watermark: None.

See above.

163

Man Seated at a Table

1970.11:151

Graphite. 6⅟₆ x 3⅝ inches (154 x 92 mm.). Irregular right margin. Verso: Graphite sketch of bearded man supporting his head with his hand. Watermark: None.

The slight sketch on the recto is perhaps a quick notation for a projected portrait; the Christ-like figure on the verso may be an idea for a religious composition.

164

Bust of a Man with His Hand on His Chin

1970.11:192

Black chalk. 5½ x 6⅞ inches (140 x 175 mm.). Several smudges of red chalk. Watermark: Coat-of-arms surmounted by crown (close to Heawood 446, 1780–87).

This spirited portrait of a middle-aged man, evidently not too much concerned with his appearance as his bristly, stringy hair suggests, is impressive by reason of his penetrating gaze. This sketch is another good example of West's ability to catch a man's personality with a few expressive lines.

165

Man with Hand on His Chin
1970.11:256

Pen and brown ink. 2⅞ x 3⅞ inches (74 x 97 mm.).
Laid down. Watermark: None.

On the basis of the sitter's hairstyle and costume,
this small spontaneous pen sketch of a balding man
with sideburns, portrayed in a pensive mood,
probably dates from the early nineteenth century.

166

Head of a Bearded Man in Profile View
1970.11:264

Pen and brown ink, brown wash. 6¾ x 6½ inches
(172 x 165 mm.). Stains of brown wash. Verso: In-
scribed in pen and brown ink: *Benj.ⁿ West Esq.r P.R.A. |
14, Newman Street, | Oxford Street.* Postal stamp and
seal. Watermark: Wilmot 1805.

The man with stubbly hair and beard recalls some
of the types in the drawings on the pages of West's
sketchbook of 1790 at the Historical Society of
Pennsylvania, Philadelphia (Am 1861, Gilpin Library, pp. 11, 13, 15).

167

Four Heads in Profile
1970.11:138

Black chalk. 9 x 6⅞ inches (228 x 163 mm.). Verso:
Two additional heads in profile. Watermark: Upper
half of coat-of-arms with horn surmounted by crown
(close to Heawood 2754).

The heads in profile on the recto and verso of this
sheet may be compared with a drawing which was
shown in the 1968 exhibition at the Bernard Black
Gallery (cat. no. 33, pen and ink, 7½ x 12 inches).
Its description in the catalogue as *Heads of Men:
Studies of Expression* might also be applied to the
Morgan sheet where, however, there is a decided
element of caricature and the grotesque. In the
head at the lower left, West amusingly depicts the
inflated face of a plump musician with the mouth-
piece of his instrument between his lips.

LANDSCAPES

Only three of the landscapes in the Morgan Library's collection of West drawings have been
signed and dated by the artist: the fine study
Gnarled Tree Trunk (No. 174, 1784); the *Landscape
with Huge Tree Trunk in Foreground* (No. 155 verso,
dated 1784 on basis of portrait on recto bearing
this date); and *Weeping Rock on the River Wye* (No.
184), which is dated 13 September 1799. Two further landscapes can be dated in the late 1780's as
they occur on the verso of historical drawings, one
of which is related to West's *Burghers of Calais* of
1789. Since it was not possible to establish a
chronological order for the remaining twenty-odd
landscape drawings, they have been grouped here
with regard to medium, drawing style, and subject matter.

168

Landscape with Two Men on Horseback
1970.11:119   PLATE 90

Black chalk on gray paper. 7⅞ x 10½ inches (200 x
267 mm.). Watermark: Upper half of fleur-de-lis
within circle.

This and the following drawing, which is executed
in the same medium and is almost identical in size,
may have come from the same sketchbook as a
drawing at the British Museum which seems to
record a view of the Villa d'Este at Tivoli (198 b
10, Book of Drawings, p. 20b; black and white
chalk on gray paper, 7¹³⁄₁₆ x 10½ inches). The two
men on horseback look out over a mountain-
ringed valley that might possibly be somewhere in
Italy.

169

Landscape with Cattle
1970.11:7   PLATE 91

Black chalk on gray paper. 8 x 10½ inches (204 x 267
mm.). Slight loss at upper right corner; stain along
right margin. Watermark: Upper half of fleur-de-lis
within circle.

170

Landscape with a Bridge
1970.11:209

Black chalk on gray paper. 4$\frac{15}{16}$ x 10$\frac{1}{8}$ inches (126 x 258 mm.). Graphite smudges at lower right. Verso: Landscape with the same bridge. Watermark: Fleur-de-lis within circle.

Although this drawing evidently was cut from a larger sheet, its medium and the paper with the fleur-de-lis watermark, which is probably Italian, may indicate that it originally formed part of the same sketchbook as the two preceding studies.

171

Landscape with a Winding River
1970.11:3   PLATE 92

Pen and brown ink, brown wash, on brown paper. 12$\frac{11}{16}$ x 17$\frac{15}{16}$ inches (322 x 455 mm.). Stains of oil paint. Verso: Sketch of mountain chain in pen and brown ink. Watermark: None.

This and the following drawing may record some mountain scenery the artist encountered on the way from Italy to France and England in 1763.

172

Mountain Landscape with River and Building in Foreground
1970.11:72   PLATE 93

Pen and brown ink, and watercolor. 10 x 14$\frac{1}{4}$ inches (255 x 365 mm.). Irregular left margin. Watermark: J Whatman.

173

Mountain Village
1970.11:116   PLATE 94

Graphite. 10$\frac{1}{16}$ x 14$\frac{3}{8}$ inches (256 x 366 mm.). Inscribed by the artist in graphite at lower right: *La bonne Ville*. Watermark: None.

This small mountain village, located in the heart of the Haute-Savoie and in the vicinity of Lake

Fig. 43   Bonneville (Savoy), Main Square.

Geneva, was given the name La Bonne Ville by its founder in 1290; it is known today as Bonneville. The main square sketched by the artist, perhaps on his journey from Italy to France in 1763 (Galt in describing this trip mentions the fact that West came into France from Savoy, *op. cit.*, I, p. 152), still shows the houses on the right with their arcades and chimneys, the outline of the mountains against which the row of houses is silhouetted, and the eighteenth-century fountain on the left (Fig. 43). (I am indebted to Artemis Karagheusian for the photograph of the village.)

174

Gnarled Tree Trunk
1970.11:2   PLATE 96

Brush and brown wash, over black chalk, on brown paper. 25$\frac{5}{8}$ x 17$\frac{3}{4}$ inches (650 x 450 mm.). A strip of paper about three inches wide was added by the artist at the bottom. The drawing on this strip is executed in a more reddish shade of brown watercolor than that used in the upper part. Signed and dated in black chalk at lower left: *B. West 1784*. Watermark: None.

This large finished landscape drawing belongs to a group of drawings from nature, inspired perhaps by the artist's walks in Windsor Park. It is related in subject matter to two other drawings of gnarled tree trunks at the Morgan Library (Acc. Nos. 1970.11:5 and 11) and two sketches of Herne's Oak, the famous ancient tree mentioned in Shakespeare's play *The Merry Wives of Windsor*, one at the Boston Museum, signed and dated *Windsor 1788* (Acc. No. 42.596; Fig. 44), the other also at the Morgan Library (Acc. No. 1970.11:144r). West loved these weather-beaten old trees and was distressed when Herne's Oak was cut down by "barbarian hands" in February 1795 as is attested by the inscription in his own hand on one of his drawings at the Folger Shakespeare Library in Washington, D.C. (cs909).

The present drawing, so appealing in its feeling for nature, was possibly derived from earlier sketchbook notations and may be considered an independent work of art; it shows West in lighter mood than that pervading the formal, neo-classical compositions of the same period.

175

Trees in a Park

1970.11:4   PLATE 95

Black chalk, some stumping, on oatmeal paper. 11¾ x 13³⁄₁₆ inches (298 x 335 mm.). Verso: Covered with black chalk for the purpose of tracing. Watermark: Coat-of-arms with fleur-de-lis, and letters G R (Heawood 1846).

176

Knotty, Gnarled Tree

1970.11:5   PLATE 97

Black chalk. 15 x 9½ inches (380 x 242 mm.). Small loss in upper left corner. Watermark: J Whatman.

177

Landscape with Gnarled Tree Trunk in Right Foreground

1970.11:144

Black chalk on letter paper inscribed in pen and brown ink on verso: *Benjamin West Esq.* | *Newman Street.* 7⅝ x 6¼ inches (193 x 158 mm.). Watermark: Coat-of-arms with horn surmounted by crown and letters GR (close to Heawood 2754).

Fig. 44   Herne's Oak, in Windsor Little Park.
Museum of Fine Arts, Boston, Gift in Memory of John H. Sturgis by His Daughters.

178

Tree Trunk

1970.11:145

Black chalk. 7½ x 6³⁄₁₆ inches (189 x 157 mm.). Watermark: None.

179

Landscape with Sheep at a Brook

1970.11:237   PLATE 98

Black chalk on brown paper. 12⅜ x 16⅞ inches (314 x 428 mm.). Verso: Compositional sketch of rural scene. Watermark: None.

This pastoral landscape with a shepherd, driving his flock before him to a meadow near a brook, calls to mind the scenery in the background of *Jacob and Laban and His Two Daughters*, now at the Wichita Art Museum, Wichita, Kansas (it was included in the 1968 exhibition of West drawings at the Bernard Black Gallery as an "Allegory of Man," c. 1785 [*op. cit.*, no. 8, cover illustration]). Although executed in pen and ink, it shows in the background the same trees with lightly sketched, feathery foliage and some grazing animals.

180

View in a Park
1970.11:218

Black chalk. 14¼ x 21¾ inches (362 x 542 mm.). Soiled along side margins. Watermark: Coat-of-arms with fleur-de-lis surmounted by crown, and letter W [Whatman].

This delicately drawn vista, perhaps sketched in Windsor Great Park, shows a pond or river in the background and a pavilion or hunting lodge in the foreground at right. The manner in which the trees with their feathery foliage are drawn, comparable to that of *Jacob and Laban and His Two Daughters* at the Wichita Art Museum (see No. 179), suggests a date in the 1780's for this landscape.

181

Kew Bridge with the Pagoda
1970.11:12   PLATE 99

Pen and light brown ink on oatmeal paper. 4⅛ x 7⅞ inches (106 x 201 mm.). Laid down on old mount bearing ticket numbered 178 in upper left corner. Inscription in pencil on back of mount in a modern hand: *Kew Gardens with the Pagoda*. Watermark: None.

According to information kindly supplied by Mr. Edward Croft-Murray, the former Keeper of Prints and Drawings of the British Museum, the bridge depicted in this drawing is Kew Bridge seen as one looks south, from the Middlesex shore of the Thames, with the road going down toward Strand-on-the-Green on the left. This stone bridge, designed by James Paine (c. 1716–89) and built in the years 1783–89, replaced John Barnard's wooden bridge of 1758–59, and so was probably relatively new when West drew it. The buildings in mid-distance, on the other side of the river, are

those on Kew Green. Sir William Chambers' famous pagoda of 1761 is visible on the right because the trees are not yet fully grown (one certainly would not be able to see it from this point today). The completion of the bridge in 1789 furnishes a *terminus post quem* for the Morgan Library's drawing.

West depicted a somewhat similar bridge in a drawing which is now at the Friends Historical Library, Swarthmore College, Swarthmore, Pennsylvania (P.P. 139). Its measurements are near enough to suggest that it may come from the same sketchbook as the Morgan drawing. It is executed in pen and brown ink and wash, and measures 5³⁄₁₆ x 8¹⁄₁₆ (131 x 205 mm.).

182

View of a Village and Other Sketches
1970.11:208

Black chalk. Sketchbook leaf, formerly folded in center. 12¾ x 8⅛ inches (322 x 205 mm.). Verso: Sketches of foliage and a bull; a Cupid. Watermark: Monogram (similar to Heawood 3242).

This leaf, clearly once part of a sketchbook, includes a view of an English village at the edge of a river and a rough landscape sketch. The small, careful drawing of the bull on the verso is reminiscent of a detail in the painting *Chryseis Returned to Her Father* of 1777 at the New-York Historical Society, in which two animals on a miniature scale can be seen in the background. The Cupid, also on the verso, was, as noted in No. 53, possibly a preliminary sketch for West's painting *Venus Rising from the Sea*.

183

View of Wrotham, Kent
1970.11:111   PLATE 101

Graphite. Staining along right margin; slight loss at upper right corner. 7 x 10½ inches (178 x 266 mm.). Inscribed by the artist in graphite at lower left: *Wrootham Kent*. The number 73 in graphite appears at the upper left corner. Watermark: Strasburg Lily (similar to Churchill 414).

This charming landscape, made by the artist on

one of his trips in the English countryside, shows the draughtsman seated at a bend in the road, sketchbook in hand. The carefully drawn foliage as well as the contrast of light and dark achieved by the lighter strokes of the pencil, for example, in the rocks, and the heavier lines, in the shrubs, are also found in three drawings in the collection of Mr. and Mrs. Paul Mellon. Possibly part of the same sketchbook as the Morgan leaf, these measure roughly 7 x 9 inches, having perhaps been trimmed a little on either side. The names of the individual villages or towns have been carefully recorded by the artist at the bottom of each of the Morgan and Mellon sheets.

Fig. 45   French Peasantry.
Museum of Fine Arts, Boston, Gift in Memory of John H. Sturgis by His Daughters.

184

Weeping Rock on the River Wye

1970.11:115   PLATE 100

Graphite. Irregular left margin. 9⅟₁₆ x 7⅜ inches (230 x 187 mm.). Inscribed by the artist in graphite at upper left: *Weeping Rock | on the river Wye – Sep.ᵗ 13. 1799 –* [the 13 of the date has been superimposed in pen over the original 15].

West visited Tintern Abbey in 1798 in the company of the Duke of Norfolk and friends as is attested by a painting *A Visit to Tintern Abbey* (signed and dated, *B. West, 1798*), which was exhibited at the Pennsylvania Academy of Fine Arts, Philadelphia, in 1938 as no. 49 and sold at auction by Parke-Bernet Galleries in 1971 (*Old Master and English Paintings*, 20 May 1971, p. 91, no. 97, illus.). This famous ruin of a gothic church is situated on the west bank of the river Wye, and West may have visited it again in September 1799. On his way to the Abbey or returning from there, he may have sketched this picturesque ledge with its rush of water. The lower Wye valley is one of the most scenic parts of England and this sketch affords a glimpse of the natural beauty along its river banks.

185

Landscape with Harvesting Peasants

1970.11:117   PLATE 102

Black chalk. 4½ x 7¼ inches (113 x 185 mm.). Watermark: None.

This and the following drawing, of identical size and medium, as well as two additional small sketches (Nos. 187–88) showing peasants gathering fruits or vegetables into a basket, may have been made by West on his trip to or from Paris in the fall of 1802 (see Nos. 161–62). A finished drawing at the Boston Museum of Fine Arts (Acc. No. 42.594; black and white chalk on blue paper, 4⅜ x 6¹³⁄₁₆ inches. Fig. 45), which is inscribed on the back of the old mount "*French Peasantry. One of the Sketches which Mr. West made in France in 1802*," shows one peasant on horseback holding a huge basket in front of him, a second running along on foot, and a third at the right holding a rake and a hoe.

186

Landscape with a Lake and Farm Houses

1970.11:118   PLATE 103

Black chalk. 4⅟₁₆ x 7¼ inches (112 x 185 mm.). Watermark: None.

187

Harvest Scene

1970.11:158

Black chalk. 2 x 1¹³⁄₁₆ inches (50 x 46 mm.). Verso: Fragment of tree. Watermark: None.

This and the following small sketch were originally part of one sheet. When placed next to each other, they show a symmetrical composition with two kneeling figures in profile in the center, two figures wearing hats on the outside, and the diagonal lines of the garlands forming two equal sides of a triangle.

188

Harvest Scene
1970.11:159

Black chalk. 2⅟₁₆ x 1¹³⁄₁₆ inches (52 x 46 mm.). Verso: Fragment of tree. Watermark: None.

189

Two Peasants
1970.11:226

Black chalk. 4⅞₁₆ x 7¼ inches (112 x 185 mm.). Watermark: None.

One of the men appears to be planting or uprooting a tree while the other stands at ease with his tool over his shoulder.

190

Landscape with Figures
1970.11:200

Black chalk. 3⅝ x 7¼ inches (92 x 184 mm.). Signed in black chalk at lower left: *B. West*. Watermark: Half of a circle and date 18. . . .

This charming landscape with an arch in a garden wall and rowboats on a pond is the setting for a biblical or mythological scene. A figure in a flowing robe appears in a cloud on the right and motions to the two figures on the left. If one of them were not wearing a hat, one might interpret the scene as the expulsion from Paradise. The composition is reminiscent of pictures by the seventeenth-century landscape painters, such as Claude, Gaspar Poussin, or Elsheimer, whose idyllic groves are peopled with gods and goddesses or biblical figures. That West had studied Claude's painting method intensively is evident from passages in Farington's diary (for instance, the entries of 8 May 1799 and 8 January 1805).

191

View of Windsor Castle
1970.11:199

Black chalk. 4¾ x 9⅝ inches (122 x 245 mm.). Smudge of red chalk at upper right. Verso: Fragment of barely visible landscape drawing. Watermark: None.

This view calls to mind Paul Sandby's drawing *The Lower Ward Looking West*; the draughtsman must have been stationed in a similar spot since one of the buildings with its crenellated tower and walls, as well as part of the round tower, appears in both drawings (see A. P. Oppé, *The Drawings of Paul and Thomas Sandby in the Collection of His Majesty the King at Windsor Castle*, Oxford and London, 1947, no. 37, pl. 25).

192

Landscape with Round Temple and Waterfall
1970.11:146

Black chalk. 7¾ x 6½ inches (196 x 167 mm.). Watermark: A. Blackwell.

This and the following two loosely sketched landscapes are distinguished by medium and drawing style from the previous drawings. Sketched with broad, swift chalk lines on a heavy, rough paper, these sheets have a summary and spontaneous character. The two larger drawings, especially, show an unerring feeling for effective landscape composition.

193

Landscape with Figure Holding a Staff
1970.11:224

Black chalk. 6⅝ x 9⅞ inches (168 x 250 mm.). Watermark: None.

194

Landscape with Large Tree
1970.11:147

Black chalk. 4¹⁵⁄₁₆ x 7⅞ inches (125 x 200 mm.). Watermark: None.

MISCELLANEOUS

195

Three Views of a Dog
1970.11:150

Black chalk. 7¼ x 6 inches (190 x 153 mm.). Watermark: Lower part of Pro Patria (close to Churchill 142).

The dog represented here, probably a bitch of the mastiff family, may have belonged to West himself or to the royal family. Among West's other drawings of dogs are the pen sketch of the forequarters of a large dog at the Royal Academy, London (Jupp Cat., I, p. 100 verso; 4⁹⁄₁₆ x 6¹¹⁄₁₆ inches), and the chalk sketch of a spaniel in the British Museum, which appears in some of the paintings of Queen Charlotte and the royal children at Windsor Castle (Millar, *op. cit.*, pls. 109, 112).

196

Sketch of a Bull
1970.11:35   PLATE 105

Black chalk, on two pieces of blue paper, pasted together. 7⁹⁄₁₆ x 9¹⁄₁₆ inches (192 x 230 mm.). Horizontal crease. Signed in black chalk at lower left: *B. West*. Watermark: None.

The bull in this drawing, like the ox in the pen sketch at the Historical Society of Pennsylvania, Philadelphia (Vol. II of Benjamin West drawings, p. 6), may have been a prize specimen in a cattle breeders' competition or it may have been raised on the King's farm at Richmond. The inscription on the Philadelphia drawing, *The ox brought from Lord Warwick's Park, and shewn to His Majesty at Windsor – Jan.ʸ 1ˢᵗ 1787*, and its measurements indicated there (10 feet long and 6 feet high) leave no doubt as to that animal's distinction. The bull in the Morgan sketch likewise appears to be a superior animal which West recorded with obvious appreciation of his subject.

197

Sketch of a Fish
1970.11:104

Black chalk on three pieces of paper glued together. Both ends rounded off. 33½ x 10⅝ inches (850 x 270 mm.). Watermark: None.

The fish in this drawing—a pike, according to one sportsman's expert opinion—may have been one of West's own fishing trophies. The old catalogues, the *Supplement to La Belle Assemblée* (p. 18), as well as Galt (*Life*, II, p. 229), mention a picture *Gentlemen Fishing at Dagenham Breach Waters* in the gallery of West's London house. There also is a drawing *Fishing by the Thames*, formerly attributed to Mortimer but now given to West, at the Henry E. Huntington Library and Art Gallery, San Marino, California (no. 70.21; pen and brown ink, with wash, 13⁵⁄₁₆ x 10¹⁵⁄₁₆ inches). It seems plausible that West may have recorded "a good catch" in this drawing.

198

Coronation of the Virgin
1970.11:212

Black chalk. Sketchbook leaf. 5¹³⁄₁₆ x 3⅞ inches (148 x 99 mm.). Watermark: Fragment.

Possibly made by West in Italy after a *quattrocento* painting, this sketch combines an Assumption with the Coronation of the Virgin. The drawing style is reminiscent of a Madonna and Child after a Barocci painting in one of West's Italian sketchbooks, now in the collection of Mr. and Mrs. Paul Mellon (see Ann C. Van Devanter, "A Holy Family Attributed to Benjamin West," *Antiques*, XCVIII, November 1970, pp. 773–75, fig. 2).

199

Michelangelo's Adam from the Creation of Eve, Sistine Chapel
1970.11:244   PLATE 107

Black chalk on pinkish-brown prepared paper. Vertical crease in center. 17¼ x 22⅞ inches (438 x 580 mm.). Inscribed in black chalk: *Adam M. Angelo's*. Watermark: None.

This and the following four drawings record details of the frescoes of Michelangelo and Raphael in the Vatican, probably made by West during his student years in Italy (1760–63). They are all, with the exception of the drawing of a foot (No. 203), of the same size and may originally have been leaves of a large sketchbook.

200

Three Figures from Michelangelo's Deluge, Sistine Chapel
1970.11:245

Pen and brown ink, and black chalk on pinkish-brown prepared paper. 17⅜ x 23 inches (440 x 587 mm.). Vertical crease in center. Inscribed in pen and brown ink: *2 figures in yᵉ Deluge of M. Angelo –*. Watermark: None.

201

Two Details from Michelangelo's Last Judgment, and Holofernes, Sistine Chapel
1970.11:246

Black chalk on pinkish-brown prepared paper; the figure of Holofernes and the detail of a leg outlined in pen and brown ink. 17⅜ x 22¾ inches (443 x 580 mm.). Watermark: None.

The two details of the angel blowing a trumpet and of the arm supporting the stem of a trumpet are taken from the central group in the lower half of Michelangelo's *Last Judgment* fresco. The figure of Holofernes is found in the pendentive fresco of Judith and Holofernes on the ceiling. The leg at the extreme right of the sheet seems to be that of a *putto*.

202

The Water-Bearer, after Raphael
1970.11:248   PLATE 106

Black chalk on pinkish-brown prepared paper. A small piece of paper, 7½ x 2 inches, has been added in center of upper margin. 22¾ x 16⅝ inches (580 x 420 mm.). Watermark: None.

The figure occurs at the extreme right of Raphael's fresco *The Fire in the Borgo*, Stanza dell'Incendio, Vatican.

203

Detail of a Foot
1970.11:247

Black chalk on pinkish-brown prepared paper. 11⅜ x 10½ inches (282 x 267 mm.). Irregular upper and left margin. Watermark: None.

The foot on this fragment of a large sheet (the irregular margins suggest that it was torn off a larger piece of paper) may have been copied from one of the seated male nudes on Michelangelo's Sistine ceiling.

204

Alexander III, King of Scotland, Rescued from the Fury of a Stag by Colin Fitzgerald
1970.11:240   PLATE 108

Graphite on two pieces of paper pasted together. Creases in several places; sheet has been folded. Some stains. 19⅞ x 26½ inches (502 x 675 mm.). Verso: Tracing in black ink (?) of the drawing on the recto. Watermark: None.

Executed with a fine point and great precision down to the minutest detail, this drawing appears to be the work of a graphic artist rather than that of a draughtsman and painter. The appearance of the design on the verso seems to confirm this hypothesis. The sheet evidently was laid on a metal plate covered with a carbon-colored ground and in the process of tracing the composition on the recto through the paper onto the plate, the raised lines and strokes on the verso picked up the color of the ground.

The graphic artist responsible for this sheet was possibly Francesco Bartolozzi. In the catalogue of Bartolozzi's prints compiled by A. de Vesme and revised and augmented by A. Calabi (*Francesco*

Fig. 46 FRANCESCO BARTOLOZZI. Alexander III, King of Scotland, Rescued from the Fury of a Stag by Colin Fitzgerald. Etching. *London, British Museum.*

Bartolozzi. Catalogue des Estampes et Notice Biographique, Milan, 1928) an etching of this subject dated 1788 is listed as no. 517 on page 135. The etching illustrated here (Fig. 46) is an impression "avant la lettre" in the collection of the British Museum (1871-6-10-725; c. 17, 2 vols.). The print, combining line and stipple engraving, reproduces the large painting which West executed for Francis Humberston Mackenzie, Baron Seaforth and Mackenzie (1754–1815), a patron of the arts, in honor of his ancestor Colin Fitzgerald; the picture is now in Fortrose Town Hall, Ross-shire, Scotland. It is executed in oil on canvas and measures 12 feet 3 inches by 17 feet 3 inches. A smaller version exists in Lord Egremont's collection, Petworth House, Sussex. The *Supplement to La Belle Assemblée* of 1 July 1808 mentions "the large picture of the Death of the Stag, or the rescuing of Alexander III; for Lord Seaforth—12 feet by 18;

the drawing and painted sketch with Mr. West." The drawing may possibly be the Morgan sheet. Two paintings of the subject were exhibited at the Royal Academy, one in 1784 (no. 402), the other in 1786 (no. 148). According to a letter at the Pennsylvania Historical Society, Philadelphia, dated 1 December 1817 and addressed to Benjamin West (Galt, *Life*, folio ed., VI, p. 69), the large painting *Alexander III, King of Scotland, Rescued from the Fury of a Stag by Colin Fitzgerald*, although paid for by Lord Seaforth, had remained in West's gallery in Newman Street. Lord Seaforth's son-in-law, J. Stewart Mackenzie, M.P., the writer of the letter, informs West that Lady Mackenzie, his wife and the daughter of Lord Seaforth, has no intention of selling the painting or parting with it, but that should she change her mind, she would be happy to give the artist preference in buying it back. The composition shows the

Fig. 47   MATTHEW LIART. Cephalus Lamenting the Death of Procris. Engraving. *London, British Museum.*

King, who has fallen from his horse, fending off the stag which Colin Fitzgerald is about to spear. The scene is vaguely reminiscent of Rubens' *Lion Hunt*, of which West owned a print.

The Friends Historical Library at Swarthmore College owns a preparatory drawing for the stag in the painting (No. 108; black chalk, heightened with white, on blue paper, 17½ x 10⅛ inches).

205

Cephalus Lamenting the Death of Procris
1970.11:243

Fragment of a tracing. 14⅛ x 10¾ inches (359 x 272 mm.). Watermark: None.

This fragment and the following two tracings (Nos.

206–07) were perhaps made for transfer to the plate by the engraver rather than West. The design on this part of the sheet shows the right half of the composition (in reversed direction) of the painting of 1770, now at the Art Institute of Chicago. The engraving was made by Matthew Liart (c. 1736–c. 1782) and is dated 1771 (Fig. 47).

206

The Cave of Despair
1970.11:242

Tracing. 13¾ x 16 inches (351 x 405 mm.). Watermark: D. & C. Blauw (Heawood 3268).

The design on this sheet represents an episode from Edmund Spenser's *The Faerie Queene* (Book 1:

Fig. 48 VALENTINE GREEN. The Cave of Despair. Mezzotint. *London, British Museum.*

The Legend of the Red Cross Knight, or of Holiness) painted by West in 1772. Valentine Green executed a mezzotint after it in 1775 (Fig. 48).

207

Aegisthus Discovering the Body of Clytemnestra
1970.11:61

Tracing. 14⅜ x 22 inches (542 x 360 mm.). Design area: 10¾ x 14 inches (273 x 354 mm.). Inscribed at lower right, in graphite in an old hand: *Bis . . .* (indecipherable); in pen and brown ink: *B. Diff: S.27.N.2.* Watermark: D. & C. Blauw (Heawood 3268).

West's painting *Aegisthus Discovering the Body of Cly-* *temnestra* was exhibited at the Royal Academy in 1780 (no. 59). According to the notation in Graves, *op. cit.*, 4, p. 214, the painting was to illustrate Thomas Francklin's translation from the Greek of the tragedies of Sophocles. The painting is no longer in existence, but there are preparatory drawings for it at Swarthmore and Boston. The mezzotint by Valentine Green is dated 1786 and, according to the legend, represents Scene IV, Act V, from Sophocles' *Electra* (presentation proof at the British Museum. Fig. 49).

208

Allegory of Charity, Woman Holding a

Fig. 49 VALENTINE GREEN. Aegisthus Discovering the Body of Clytemnestra. Mezzotint. *London, British Museum.*

Child, Kneeling Woman with Veil, and Two Profiles of a Bearded Man
1970.11:261

Graphite on thin paper. 20⅞ x 13⅛ inches (535 x 335 mm.). Several creases. Watermark: J. Bigg.

The tracings on this sheet have been made from either drawings or prints. A few lines of red chalk on the verso of the profiles of the bearded man suggest they were traced from a red chalk drawing. The Charity group may be compared to the pen drawing *Allegorical Figure of Charity* by West at the Philadelphia Museum of Art (Acc. No. 39-15-1), although there a statuesque woman covers three naked children with her cloak. The second tracing on the Morgan sheet, the woman holding a child, may also be connected with the Charity group. On the other hand, the two profiles of the garlanded

bearded head, perhaps of a river god, and the woman with her billowing drapery, possibly a nymph or female deity, may relate to a mythological subject. One may perhaps postulate *seicento* models for the figures on this sheet.

209

The Orders of St. Michael and the Holy Ghost
1970.11:139

Black chalk. 4⅞ x 6½ inches (124 x 165 mm.). Inscribed in black chalk by the artist: *order of St Michael | order of Holy Ghost*. Verso: Naval trophy and inscription in pen and brown ink: *To Mʳ West*. Watermark: Pro Patria.

These sketches of the French Orders of St. Michael and of the Holy Ghost (St. Esprit) may have been made by West in connection with the portrait of some dignitary or a figure in a historical painting.

210

Heraldic Lion

1970.11:258

Black chalk on light brown paper. 7¼ x 4⅝ inches (185 x 118 mm.). Irregular left margin. Watermark: Coat-of-arms with fleur-de-lis surmounted by crown (close to Heawood 1846).

The heraldic lion in this drawing may have served as a model for the British lion in the coat-of-arms of England in one of West's historical paintings; a similar lion, only in reversed direction, appears combined with the unicorn of the English arms on top of the Speaker's chair in the compositional sketch for *Cromwell Dissolving the Long Parliament* at the Friends Historical Library, Swarthmore College (Fig. 19). In the same collection there is also the drawing of the head and forequarters of a lion (P.P. 260; pencil touched with white, 9¾ x 6¼ inches), which, however, by reason of its immediacy and realistic detail, seems to be a study from nature.

211

Roman Standard

1970.11:160

Pen and brown ink on a calling card imprinted: *M.ʳ Bryan | Putney*. 2¼ x 2⁵⁄₁₆ inches (57 x 74 mm.). Inscribed in pen and ink on cartouche: *Touch me Not*. Verso: Similar design in black chalk. Watermark: None.

212

Trident

1970.11:253

Black chalk. 6⅝ x 7³⁄₁₆ inches (169 x 183 mm.). Several creases. Inscribed in black chalk by the artist: *From M.ʳ West. Aug.ᵗ 7.ᵗʰ 1811*. Watermark: None.

Although this trident is very similar to that of Victory in West's painting *The Apotheosis of Lord Nelson* of 1807 at the National Maritime Museum, Greenwich, England, the date of 7 August 1811 indicates that this drawing must have had another purpose.

213

A Caravan or Gypsy Cart

1970.11:254

Black chalk on oatmeal paper. 4⅞ x 3⅛ inches (125 x 80 mm.). Watermark: None.

A horse-drawn caravan like that in this drawing served as living quarters for gypsies. That West was keenly interested in what he saw on his walks in the country and in London is evident from the drawings *Characters in the Streets of London*, signed and dated 1799 (now at the Berry-Hill Galleries, New York), and *A Cripple in the Streets of London* and *A Beggarman from Nature* (the latter two mentioned in the 1839 sale catalogue of West drawings, Lots 13 and 107).

Fig. 50   RAPHAEL WEST.
Hercules Slaying the Hydra. Etching.
London, British Museum.

Raphael Lamar West, 1766–1850

There is very little known about Raphael West. If it were not for the few instances in which he is mentioned by contemporary writers, notably Joseph Farington and William Dunlap, our knowledge of him would be even scantier. He stood in the shadow of his father whose assistant he was and, although not without talent, never made a name for himself. According to William T. Whitley (*Art in England 1800–1820*, New York and Cambridge, England, 1928, p. 64), Raphael applied for an associateship at the Royal Academy in 1791 but the Academy decided in favor of Thomas Lawrence. Although Raphael and his younger brother were left an estate by their father estimated at £100,000, Raphael exhausted his share and had to appeal to the Academy for financial help, which was given (Whitley, *op. cit.*, p. 311). There are several of Raphael's requests for money addressed to his father among the Benjamin West papers at the Historical Society of Pennsylvania, Philadelphia. In one of the earlier letters in the same collection written by a certain Henry Sulger to Mrs. West and dated 15 August 1774, Raphael (then eight years old) is referred to as the "infant genius." According to Mrs. West's own testimony, her husband's "easy temper had caused Him to allow His sons to be brought up improvidently. They could contribute nothing to lessen His expenses" (Farington, *Diary*, entry of 5 May 1807). The painter and writer on art Charles Robert Leslie probably described Raphael's problem most aptly when he said in a letter to his friend William Dunlap, "You know our friend Raphael possessed more talent than industry" (W. Dunlap, *History of the Rise and Progress of the Arts of Design in the United States*, rev. ed., 1965, II, p. 290).

COMPOSITIONS AND FIGURES

214

Cadmus Slaying the Dragon

1970.11:53   PLATE 109

Pen and brown ink, over graphite. 11¾ x 8⅞ inches (297 x 225 mm.). Watermark: None.

The attribution of this drawing to Raphael West is made on the basis of its close relationship in composition and drawing style with the etching *Hercules Slaying the Hydra* which is signed and dated *R. L. West 1785* (the impression at the British Museum measures 15⅛ x 12 inches; 40-3-14-174. Fig. 50). There are two more drawings in the same style, *Cadmus Slaying the Dragon* at the Whitworth Art Gallery, Manchester, England (pen and brown ink, pencil and wash, 21⅞ x 17⅛ inches. Fig. 51), and *Hercules and Antaeus* at the Morgan Library (1973.2. Gift of Mrs. Iola S. Haverstick; pen and brown ink, over black chalk, 10 x 8¹⁄₁₆ inches. Fig. 52). The subject of the Whitworth sheet is more clearly identifiable as Cadmus slaying the dragon than in the Morgan drawing since Cadmus' dead companions, who were killed by the beast when

Fig. 51 RAPHAEL WEST.
Cadmus Slaying the Dragon.
Manchester, England, Whitworth Art Gallery.

they approached his cave in search of water, appear in the foreground; Cadmus in the Whitworth drawing is seen poised to slay the dragon with a javelin—in accordance with the story in Ovid's *Metamorphoses* in which the hero first hurls a massive stone—without result—and then uses a javelin which penetrates the scales and deals the fatal blow (Ovid, *Metamorphoses*, The Loeb Classical Library, I, Book III, pp. 125–31).

John Trumbull, the American painter, noted in his autobiography that on 12 August 1786 he went to Versailles and saw there among other famous paintings "three Labors of Hercules, by Guido, very fine; that with the hydra almost the same as Raph [sic] West's etching; the upper part perfectly the same" (*The Autobiography of Colonel John Trumbull*, ed. by Theodore Sizer, New York, 1970, p. 112). Raphael West obviously must have seen Reni's painting, which is now at the Louvre (see Cesare Gnudi, *Guido Reni*, 1955, pl. 87), or, more likely, an engraving after it.

215

Orlando Rescuing Oliver from the Lion
1970.11:10   PLATE 110

Pen and brown ink. 9 x 12⅛ inches (229 x 306 mm.). Verso: Three sketches of heads in graphite (head of a woman in a bonnet and two grotesque male heads). Watermark: Coat-of-arms with horn surmounted by crown and letters G R.

This and the following two drawings were executed by Raphael West in connection with John Boydell's ambitious Shakespeare Gallery project. Originally, thirty-five artists were to contribute 170 paintings, but—as it turned out later—nearly half of the paintings were executed by four artists: William Hamilton, Smirke, Westall, and Wheatley. The Gallery opened in Pall Mall in June 1789 with thirty-four paintings. However, this huge undertaking brought the Boydells (John and his nephew Josiah) close to bankruptcy and by Act of Parliament the firm was permitted in 1804 to sell 22,000 three-guinea lottery tickets. The holder of the sixty-second ticket, a Mr. Tassie, was the lucky winner of, among other privileges, all the pictures from Shakespeare, large and small. In the end, the pictures were sold at Christie's on 17–19 May 1805 (see W. Moelwyn Merchant, *Shakespeare and the*

Artist, London, 1959, pp. 66–76). According to Algernon Graves (*Art Sales*, III, London, 1921, p. 327), at this sale three paintings by Benjamin West, *Ophelia, before the King and Queen, Orlando and Oliver*, and *King Lear in the Storm*, were bought by "Robert Fulton, for Philadelphia."

The Morgan Library's drawing is preparatory for the painting *Orlando and Oliver* which, as W. Moelwyn Merchant states (*op. cit.*, p. 239), was deposited by Robert Fulton with the two other Benjamin West paintings at the Pennsylvania Academy for exhibition, but in September 1816 Mrs. Fulton in New York demanded they be returned to her. Since the present location of the painting is not known, an impression of the engraving by William Charles Wilson at the British Museum furnishes an idea of the painting's composition (D.D.6, No. 31, Vol. I, c 17*. Fig. 53); the legend on the engraving, "Painted by Raphael West," and the publication date, 1 December 1798, identify the true author of the painting and the time of its execution. The composition represents Act IV, Scene III, of *As You Like It* when Orlando rescues Oliver from the lion and the serpent. Raphael West's

Fig. 52 RAPHAEL WEST.
Hercules and Antaeus.
New York, Pierpont Morgan Library, Gift of Mrs. Iola S. Haverstick.

Fig. 53 WILLIAM CHARLES WILSON. As You Like It, Act IV, Scene III. Engraving. *London, British Museum.*

friend and exact contemporary William Dunlap, in his *History of the Rise and Progress of the Arts of Design . . .* (first published in 1834, rev. ed., New York, 1965, I, p. 285, and II, p. 289), confirms the attribution to Raphael West.

The Morgan drawing shows a composition similar to that of the engraving, though the poses are different. The figure of Oliver in the engraving, with its impetuous forward motion, clearly reveals its indebtedness to Salvator Rosa's Jason in his etching *Jason and the Dragon* (Bartsch 18). It is interesting to note in this connection that a picture of "Jason and the Dragon—in imitation of Salvator Rosa" is mentioned among Benjamin West's pictures in the *Supplement to La Belle Assemblée* (p. 17).

There was another preparatory drawing by Raphael West for the Orlando composition formerly in Harry Margary's possession (Professor von Erffa kindly provided this information).

216

Sketches for a Recumbent Figure

1970.11:193   PLATE 111

Graphite on oatmeal paper. 9⅜ x 14¾ inches (239 x 375 mm.). Smudges of red chalk along upper, lower, and right margins. Watermark: None.

This drawing and another at the Philadelphia Museum of Art (Acc. No. 67-153-3; graphite, 5 x 7½ inches. Fig. 54) are preparatory studies for the scene in *As You Like It* where the sleeping Oliver is attacked by a "green and gilded snake" and by a lioness when he was resting under an oak, whose "boughs were moss'd with age." The rather developed sketch near the lower margin of the Morgan sheet and the youth encircled by the snake in the forest scenery of the Philadelphia drawing are close to the figure in the print after Raphael's painting.

Fig. 54   RAPHAEL WEST.
Oliver Attacked by a Snake.
Philadelphia, Philadelphia Museum of Art,
Given by The Robert L. McNeil, Jr., Trusts.

217

Brigand Lying under a Tree
1970.11:8   PLATE 112

Pen and brown ink, over black chalk. 15 x 10⅜ inches
(380 x 259 mm.). Loss at upper left corner. Verso
covered with red chalk for the purpose of tracing.
Watermark: Coat-of-arms with horn surmounted by
crown and letters G R.

This and the following pen sketch are preparatory
drawings for the etching signed *R. L. West*, an impression of which is at the British Museum (1925-
5-11-166; plate size: 16¼ x 11¹¹⁄₁₆ inches. Fig. 55).
The composition appears in the opposite direction
in the print. The revival of the themes of Salvator
Rosa (soldiers and bandits in a landscape setting)
which appealed to Raphael West and many artists
of his generation signals—together with other phe-
nomena, especially a new feeling for nature—the
advent of the Romantic period.

218

Brigand Lying under a Tree
1970.11:9   PLATE 113

Pen and brown ink. 7¾ x 10⅟₁₆ inches (196 x 255 mm.).
Verso covered with red chalk for the purpose of tracing. Watermark: Fragment of fleur-de-lis.

This sketch of a young man lying under a tree,
with his head supported by his left hand, may have
been Raphael West's first idea for the figure in the

Fig. 55   RAPHAEL WEST.
Brigand Lying under a Tree. Etching.
London, British Museum.

British Museum print (Fig. 55). Another drawing,
formerly on the New York art market, shows two
studies of the head and two round objects, perhaps
cannonballs. See also Fig. 64.

219

The Creation of Eve (?)
1970.11:25   PLATE 114

Pen and brown ink. 6⅝ x 9 inches (168 x 229 mm.).
Watermark: None.

Although the group at right might be interpreted
as God the Father creating Eve from one of
Adam's ribs, the presence of an angel with large
wings pointing heavenward is rather unusual. The
rather attractive finished drawing has all the characteristics of Raphael West's drawing style: the
somewhat superficial and sketchy anatomy of the

figures, the old gnarled trees of the landscape setting, and the extensive use of parallel and cross hatchings. The figures with their bushy hair and flat, insubstantial limbs can hardly be distinguished from the dead tree branches and become part of the forest landscape.

220

Aeneas and the Cumaean Sibyl

1970.11:14   PLATE 115

Pen and brown ink, brown wash, black and white chalk on brown paper. 12⅝ x 15 inches (320 x 281 mm.). Verso: Kneeling figure in black chalk, the face gone over with pen and ink, and head of horse in pen and ink, also profile of a man. Watermark: None.

The subject of this drawing is perhaps taken from Virgil's *Aeneid*, Book VI. Aeneas descends with the Sibyl to the netherworld where they encounter the ghosts of the dead, among them that of Aeneas' father, Anchises, and of Dido. The apparition on the right, floating on clouds—if it really is a female ghost—may be that of the late Queen of Carthage who committed suicide when deserted by Aeneas. The outlines of the Cumaean Sibyl's cave and of a temple with columns, perhaps symbolizing Rome, can be seen in the background. The sketchy manner in which the figures are outlined is similar to the rather crude pen work of the following drawing.

221

Sketch for "Macbeth" (Act I, Scene III)

1970.11:37   PLATE 115

Pen and brown ink over graphite on oatmeal paper. 10⁹⁄₁₆ x 14¹¹⁄₁₆ inches (269 x 372 mm.). Watermark: None.

Although the old catalogues of Benjamin West's *oeuvre* mention "The Sketch of Macbeth and the Witches" (the *Supplement to La Belle Assemblée* lists it among the pictures painted by Mr. West for his own collection and located in the Painting-room), the identification of this drawing with this painting must remain doubtful, especially in view of the fact that to date no painting or print of the subject has turned up.

The drawing, which is an illustration of Act I, Scene III, of *Macbeth*, is here attributed to Raphael West on the basis of its drawing style—the broken, scratchy pen lines evidently set down with great impatience by a temperamental artist, who nevertheless convincingly evokes the ominous encounter of Macbeth and Banquo with the three witches on the heath. The same drawing style can be found in the *Arrest of Christ* and the *Angel at the Tomb* (Nos. 222–23) and in several landscapes (Nos. 247–48).

222

The Arrest of Christ

1970.11:19

Pen and brown ink on oatmeal paper. 6⅝ x 10⅝ inches (170 x 268 mm.). Irregular margins on three sides. Upper left corner repaired. Verso: Sketch in graphite (unidentifiable). Watermark: None.

This and the following drawing—both executed in the same medium and of almost identical size—show two scenes from the New Testament in Raphael West's rough outline technique. *The Arrest of Christ*, with Peter visible on the right pulling out his sword, is a very typical example of his improvisational performance. The rather crude sketch of the child holding a dog on a leash at lower left adds a lighter touch to the grim event of Christ's imprisonment—evidently a night-piece.

223

The Angel Announcing the Resurrection to the Marys

1970.11:18

Pen and brown ink, over graphite, on oatmeal paper. 6⅜ x 10⅜ inches (162 x 265 mm.). Irregular lower margin. Stain at lower right. Verso: Inscribed in pen and brown ink: *In | 16 – by – 24 | 12 – by 16*. Watermark: None.

The angel hovering on the rock covering the sepulchre seems to be indebted, in pose and gesture, to the same figure in Benjamin West's painting *The Angel of the Lord Announcing the Resurrection to the Marys at the Sepulchre* of 1805, now at the Brooklyn Museum (Evans, *West*, pl. 3) and to his lithograph

Fig. 56 BENJAMIN WEST.
The Angel at the Tomb of Christ. Lithograph.
New York, New York Public Library, Astor, Lennox and Tilden Foundations, Prints Division.

Fig. 57 BENJAMIN WEST.
Madre Dolorosa.
Formerly New York, Metropolitan Museum of Art (Photograph Courtesy Frick Art Reference Library).

signed and dated *B. West 1801*, an impression of which is in the Joseph Pennell collection at the New York Public Library (Fig. 56). The rising sun and the two women shielding their eyes with their hands from the radiance of the angel point to the fact that the drawing is an interpretation of Matthew XXVIII, "... In the end of the sabbath, as it began to dawn toward the first day of the week, came Mary Magdalene and the other Mary to see the sepulchre...."

224

The Virgin and the Dead Christ
1970.11:141   PLATE 116

Pen and brown ink. 7⅜ x 5⁷⁄₁₆ inches (189 x 139 mm.). Irregular upper margin. Verso: Fragment of the draft of a letter by Raphael Lamar West offering, on behalf of himself and his brother, Benjamin West, Jr., their father's paintings to the government of the United

States; inscribed in pen and brown ink by the same hand along left margin: *6-by-7-½ feet*. Watermark: . . . N HALL (according to Churchill, 1829).

This rough outline drawing of the Virgin with the body of Christ brings to mind in its general scheme the painting *Madre Dolorosa* signed and dated *B. West 1798*, formerly at the Metropolitan Museum of Art (Bryson Burroughs, *Catalogue of Paintings, The Metropolitan Museum of Art*, New York, 1920, p. 328, w52-5. Fig. 57); the picture was de-accessioned by the museum and sold at Parke-Bernet on 27 March 1956 (Lot 36). The Morgan drawing, like the draft of the letter on its verso, was probably executed much later than 1798, probably shortly before 1826; it does, however, seem to reflect Benjamin West's 1798 composition in the relationship of the two figures, and the type and facial expression of the Virgin. The painting, formerly at the Metropolitan Museum of Art, may be related to *The Virgin and the Dead Christ*, one of the pictures Benjamin West painted for William Beckford and Fonthill Abbey. The date 1798 on the painting tends to support this assumption since Benjamin West and his son Raphael were both at Fonthill in the summer of that year. *A Description of Fonthill Abbey, Wiltshire,* of 1812, by James Storer, mentions "a Pietà by West" as in "the dressing room towards the west, underneath Mantegna's famous *Christ on the Mount of Olives,* now at the National Gallery, London." The Beckford picture was included in the sale at Christie's (*Magnificent Effects at Fonthill Abbey, Wilts.,* 1–11 October 1822, p. 52, no. 21).

The fragmentary draft of the letter on the verso of the Morgan drawing is interesting in its revelation of the total amount that West's sons desired to realize from the sale of their father's paintings. The sum of £40,000 was to be paid either in annuities or, if this should not be agreeable, they would require a down payment of £12,000 "which is absolutely necessary" and take the remainder in American stock. The actual letter, dated 12 April 1826, and addressed to the Speaker of the House of Representatives, the Hon. J. W. Taylor, by West's sons, was made part of the Congressional Record (19th Congress, 2d Session, Document No. 8). This letter offering to the government of the United States one hundred and fifty paintings by Benjamin West does not mention any sum of money; there is, however, a list of one hundred and fifty paintings attached to it which, as the brothers suggest, "may form the foundation of a school for the growth of the fine arts in the rapidly advancing States of America" or present "an opportunity of commencing a truly National Gallery." (In this connection, it may be recalled that the National Gallery in London had been founded just two years earlier in 1824.) Document No. 8 was read in the House of Representatives on 11 December 1826. The decision reached was evidently negative since all the paintings offered here appear again in George Robins' sale catalogue of 1829. Whitley in *Art in England, 1821–1837* (pp. 168–71) states that "according to published statements, West's pictures realized altogether 19,137 guineas" (about £20,000) and that "to West's sons and heirs, Raphael and Benjamin, the sale must have been intensely disappointing. They realized nothing like the prices expected, or what they could have been sold for, while West was alive." As a matter of fact, the two brothers were in straitened circumstances and had to appeal twice to the Royal Academy for financial assistance, which was given.

225

St. Michael

1970.11:103   PLATE 117

Graphite. Squared and numbered for transfer. 26½ x 17¼ inches (672 x 436 mm.). Repairs at upper left corner and in center of upper margin. Some foxing. Watermark: None.

The fierce, muscular warrior in a plumed helmet, seated on a rock and holding shield and spear—characterized only by his wings as one of the archangels—appears almost exactly identical though in reverse direction in a drawing at the Henry E. Huntington Library and Art Gallery, San Marino, which is signed *R. L. West* (graphite, 25 x 16½ inches; Christie's sale of 14 March 1967, p. 13, lot 53, illus.). The two drawings differ only in minor details; for instance, the Morgan sheet does not show the straps with which the shield is attached to the warrior's arm in the Huntington Library's drawing; on the other hand, the strand of hair falling over St. Michael's right arm and the clouds which are seen in the background of the Morgan drawing are missing in the Huntington Library's sheet. The Morgan drawing, undoubtedly, was intended either for a painting or a print as the squaring and numbers indicate.

226

Shipwreck Scene

1970.11:36   PLATE 118

Pen and black ink, gray wash. Arched top. 6¾6 x 16¹³⁄₁₆ inches (173 x 427 mm.). Some red chalk at upper right. Inscribed on verso in pen and brown ink: *B.. West;* fragment of seal. Watermark: J Whatman.

Although a very finished drawing such as this is rather unusual in the Morgan group of Raphael West drawings, the broken, nervous pen lines, the parallel hatchings, and the strong outlining of the figures point to him as the draughtsman. The irregularly cut, arched top—if it is not due to some accident—may indicate that the design was perhaps intended to fill some architectural space. The subject may be compared with *The Deluge* by Joshua Shaw, an American painter of Raphael West's generation, at the Metropolitan Museum of Art (Gardner and Feld, *op. cit.*, I, p. 133), where the artist also depicted a natural catastrophe with similarly foaming waves.

227

Standing Male Nude Seen from the Back
1970.11:23   PLATE 119

Pen and brown ink, over black chalk. 18¾ x 10⅜ inches (447 x 262 mm.). Verso: Black chalk sketch of nude warrior with helmet slaying man with a sword, and fragment of another sketch. Watermark: None.

228

Male Nude Wrestling (?)
1970.11:134   PLATE 119

Black chalk, some lines gone over with the pen and black ink. 7⅝ x 4¾ inches (193 x 121 mm.). Watermark: None.

229

Male Torso with Raised Right Arm
1970.11:132

Black chalk. 6½ x 5⅝ inches (165 x 143 mm.). Watermark: J Whatman.

230

Fallen Nude Man in Distress
1970.11:130

Black chalk. 6½ x 8⅜ inches (165 x 208 mm.). Watermark: Upper half of VII.

231

Study for an Execution (Cain Slaying Abel?)
1970.11:51

Pen and brown ink on oatmeal paper. 9⅚ x 7½ inches (250 x 198 mm.). Watermark: None.

The following drawing as well as three others in various collections may be related to the present compositional sketch. The drawing which is closest to the two Morgan drawings is that now at the Black-Nadeau Gallery, Monte Carlo (formerly at Spink's, London; originally from Mrs. Claire Francis' collection; for illustration, see *Burlington Magazine*, CIX, August 1967, p. XI). It shows a more careful study of the group seen in the Morgan drawing except that the figure holding the weapon is nude and the kneeling victim is drawn in a slightly different pose. Two anatomically more detailed drawings of the figure with the club were included in the 1968 West exhibition at the Bernard Black Gallery (cat. nos. 26 and 27. Figs. 58, 59).

There is a very rough compositional sketch of another execution scene on the verso of No. 259.

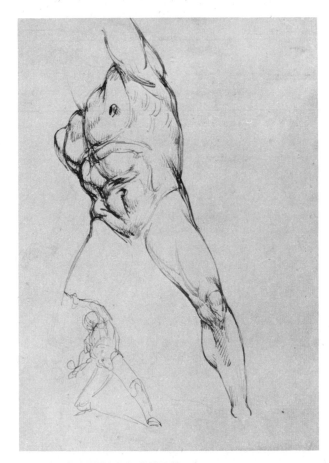

Fig. 58   RAPHAEL WEST.
Study for an Execution.
Formerly New York, Bernard Black Gallery.

232

Four Studies for an Execution
1970.11:178

Pen and brown ink. 9⁷⁄₁₆ x 8 inches (239 x 203 mm.). Irregular right margin. Verso: Two studies for a kneeling figure. Watermark: Coat-of-arms with fleur-de-lis surmounted by crown.

The four rapidly sketched figures on the recto and those on the verso of this sheet may have been made by the artist in preparation for the composition of the preceding drawing. There is a further sheet with two kneeling figures in the collection of Mr. and Mrs. Paul Mellon (Fig. 60). The Black-Nadeau drawing mentioned in the preceding entry, as well as the Mellon sketches, show the kneeling figure in a helpless suppliant's pose in contrast to the figure in the Morgan compositional sketch (No. 231) who grasps the leg of the assailant in an effort to stop him.

233

Three Men Crushed under a Large Rock
1970.11:128
Graphite. 10⁹⁄₁₆ x 13 inches (269 x 330 mm.). Watermark: None.

234

Man Peering over a Rock
1970.11:129
Black chalk. Eye, nose, and mouth of the figure have been gone over with pen and brown-black ink. 11 ⅛ x 7¾ inches (283 x 197 mm.). Watermark: Letter W [Whatman].

Fig. 60 RAPHAEL WEST.
Two Kneeling Figures.
Collection of Mr. and Mrs. Paul Mellon, Upperville, Virginia.

Fig. 59 RAPHAEL WEST.
Study for an Execution.
Formerly New York, Bernard Black Gallery.

Fig. 61 RAPHAEL WEST.
Two Figures in a Landscape.
Formerly New York, Bernard Black Gallery.

Since the figure appears to be one-eyed, he may well represent the Cyclops Polyphemus.

235

Falling Male Nude
1970.11:95

Pen and brown ink. 6½ x 7¹¹⁄₁₆ inches (165 x 195 mm.). Verso: Rough compositional sketch of an assassination scene, and of a prostrate figure. Watermark: None.

LANDSCAPES

236

Two Men in a Landscape Setting
1970.11:238

Pen and brown ink. 7⅛ x 8¹⁵⁄₁₆ inches (180 x 227 mm.). Watermark: 1811.

This variant of the many execution scenes drawn by Raphael, perhaps a representation of Cain and Abel, is very similar in size and medium to the drawing of the same subject entitled "Despair" in the catalogue of the 1968 Bernard Black Gallery exhibition (no. 28, 7⅛ x 7¼ inches. Fig. 61).

237

View of the Town of Geneva on Seneca Lake
1970.11:110   PLATE 120

Pen and black ink. 8 x 13 inches (202 x 330 mm.). Extensive losses along upper margin and lower left, the lower right corner is missing, numerous tears and extraneous spots of brown color. Watermark: E Wilding 1794.

This drawing and the following four, possibly also two further sheets, relate to the trip Raphael West made to America at the close of the eighteenth century. Boyd Alexander in his biography of William Beckford (*England's Wealthiest Son*, London, 1962, p. 219) reports that Benjamin West and his fellow American artist John Trumbull (1756–1843) had persuaded Beckford, the author of *Vathek*, to buy land in America, and in August 1798 Raphael was sent overseas to act as Beck-

ford's agent. Alexander suggests that the property in question was perhaps that which West himself owned, having purchased it from the well-known educator James Wadsworth (1768–1844), and which he now hoped to sell to Beckford at a profit. Raphael's eyewitness report on the property in 1802 was negative, and as a result Beckford did not pay over the money and was prevented from making a bad investment at the "monstrous" price reported by Joseph Farington in his diary (I, p. 251) of ten shillings an acre for the vast tract of around twenty-five thousand acres.

Raphael West's sketchbook recording this expedition into the wilderness of northwestern New York State, more particularly the region of the Genesee River, is now in the Library of Rutgers University, New Brunswick, New Jersey. On folio 7 is a partial view of the town of Geneva on Seneca Lake, one of the Finger Lakes, which, except for minor details, is identical with that in the present drawing. Two other drawings in the Morgan Library's collection (Nos. 239–40) are closely related to the Rutgers sketchbook leaves: folio 3 shows the same view of Honeyoye Lake, another of the Finger Lakes, as does No. 239, and folio 4 the same two log cabins surrounded by barren tree trunks and stumps that are represented in No. 240. The latter drawing, as a matter of fact, shows only the left half of the view in the Rutgers sketchbook which is inscribed along the upper margin: *Big tree Gennesee River. Mr. Wadsworth's*. Another Morgan drawing, identified by the artist as *The Hotel at the Catskill Mountains – North America*, shows a group of buildings overlooking a mountain lake or stream (No. 238); the artist and his wife, Maria, née Siltso, whom he had married only shortly before embarking on this trip, may have spent a night or two here during their travels. The above Morgan sheets are outline drawings while those in the sketchbook give more detail and convey a better idea of the scenery. The inscription on the verso of No. 239 suggests that from these drawings Raphael traced copies to be sent to his father in England. Among other drawings connected with Raphael's trip to America are *Forest and Swamp* in the Minneapolis Institute of Arts (68.53.1), *Lower Falls of the Genesee River* at the Munson-Williams-Proctor Institute, Utica, New York, and *A Log Cabin in a Forest Clearing* in a New York private collection (formerly Leger Galleries Ltd., London).

William Dunlap (1766–1839), the American painter, engraver, and writer on art, in his *History of the Rise and Progress of the Arts of Design in the United States* of 1834 (rev. ed., 1965, II, pp. 286–91) reports that "of all creatures my friend Raphael was the least fitted for the task of a pioneer in America." He also tells the story of Raphael West's surprise when he sat drawing at a lower window in Wadsworth's house at Big Tree and a bear marched up to him "as if to take a lesson."

238

The Hotel at the Catskill Mountains
1970.11:81   PLATE 121

Pen and black ink, some black chalk (clouds). 7¼ x 8¹⁵⁄₁₆ inches (184 x 228 mm.). Design area: 4¾ x 7⅛ inches (121 x 180 mm.). Inscribed by the artist in black chalk below lower margin: *The Hotel at the Catskill Mountains – North America.*

See No. 237.

239

View of Honeyoye Lake
1970.11:82   PLATE 121

Pen and brown ink. 3⅝ x 6¹³⁄₁₆ inches (93 x 173 mm.). Ink stain, four small perforations. Inscribed by the artist in brown ink above design: *A view of the head on Inlet of Honeyoye Lake – the diversity of tint on | these hills is Beauutifull. the land at the | other end of the lake if of the Best quality | & purfectly Flat for miles.* Inscribed by the artist on verso in brown ink along upper margin: *I traced those I sent to England For my Father | May 8ᵗʰ 1799.*

See No. 237.

240

Landscape with Log Cabins near the Genesee River
1970.11:6   PLATE 120

Pen and dark brown ink. 3¾ x 3½ inches (96 x 90 mm.). Three small perforations as made by a pin or pins.

See No. 237.

241

Landscape with Log Cabin, Farmer and Pig
1970.11:106   PLATE 122

Watercolor over preliminary indications in black chalk. 5¾ x 7¹⁵⁄₁₆ inches (145 x 200 mm.).

242

Landscape with Farm House and Farmer near a Pond
1970.11:107   PLATE 122

Watercolor. 5¹¹⁄₁₆ x 7¹³⁄₁₆ inches (145 x 199 mm.).

This pair of sketchbook leaves, which are almost identical in size, may represent rural scenes in North America at the close of the eighteenth century or the beginning of the nineteenth. Raphael West perhaps recorded them during his exploratory trip to the Genesee valley in 1798–1802 or executed them on the basis of sketchbook notations after his return to England. These two watercolors as well as two more, one in the Morgan Library's collection (No. 243) and another formerly at the Leger Galleries Ltd. in London, now in a New York private collection, are very similar to the drawing of log cabins and trees on the pages of the Raphael West sketchbook in the Library of Rutgers University.

243

Landscape with Lake and Fallen Trees in the Foreground
1970.11:108   PLATE 123

Pen and black ink, watercolor. Two vertical creases running parallel with right margin. 9⅞ x 14¹³⁄₁₆ inches (252 x 375 mm.). Watermark: C. Pike 1802. Inscribed in graphite on verso: *Philadelphia as it was when [R L West visited America crossed out] B Wests time | so I was told | T Margary.*

This landscape, which may be compared with the view *Part of Lake Ontario* in Raphael West's sketchbook at Rutgers University, may have been executed in watercolor after the artist's return to England in 1802. The date of the paper seems to support this assumption. The partial view of Lake

Ontario in the sketchbook, although drawn with pen and ink, shows the same flat landscape with uprooted trees in the foreground in reversed direction. The present drawing is an apt illustration of the text in the sketchbook describing the "sandy beach of Ontario" as "covered with bleached & weatherbeaten Fragments of trees, brought down the Rivers in the spring. . . ." It also shows the same russet shades of watercolor as the two sketchbook leaves discussed in the preceding entries.

The person responsible for the inscription on the verso—Raphael West's son-in-law, Thomas George Margary, who crossed out the phrase "[when] R L West visited America" and changed it to read "Philadelphia as it was [in] B Wests time"—appears to have been mistaken as to the location depicted in the drawing. The inscription, which must have been added after Raphael West's death in 1850, was obviously based on hearsay.

244

Mountain Lake with Small Sailboats
1970.11:113

Pen and gray ink. 10⅛ x 14⅛ inches (255 x 360 mm.). Inscribed in graphite on verso by a modern hand: *Mountain Lake in America.* Watermark: Lower portion of coat-of-arms with fleur-de-lis surmounted by crown and letter W [Whatman].

245

The Forest God
1970.11:67   PLATE 124

Pen and black ink and reddish-brown and tan watercolor. 9⅞ x 14⅞ inches (251 x 378 mm.). Watermark: Coat-of-arms with fleur-de-lis surmounted by crown and monogram PG.

This and the following drawing can probably be connected with Raphael West's stay in America (1799–1802), since a poem jotted down in his American sketchbook of 1799–1800 at the Rutgers University Library seems to be the literary basis for this visual fantasy:

"There (midst the Wilderness, all drenched
    & damp,
  Tergrown with moss, immersed in swamp,

Were neither Autumn glows, nor Spring
    can Bloom,
  Buryed with Earth & Waters deep in gloom)
    Dwells in Eternal Solitude,
      The Forrest God. . . ."

The poet added below these lines: "The Savages of North America believe in a Great Spirit inhabiting their Forrests."

Fig. 62   RAPHAEL WEST.
"The Forest God." Lithograph.
London, British Museum.

Fig. 63   Here attributed to BENJAMIN WEST, JR.
Bagshot Heath, Surrey.
*Museum of Fine Arts, Boston, Gift in Memory of
John H. Sturgis by His Daughters.*

A related lithograph at the British Museum, signed and dated *R. L. West. 1802*, shows the head of a bearded man, the Forest God of the poem and the Morgan drawings, oak branches and leaves framing his fierce countenance, his eyes glaring from the shadow of his brow (52-2-14-211; 10½ x 8½ inches. Fig. 62). Although this and the following smaller drawing must have been executed by Raphael West after his return to England (see watermark of 1805 below), the virgin forests of North America, with their Indian lore and all kinds of wild beasts, undoubtedly fired Raphael West's imagination in this composition.

246

The Forest God
1970.11:68

Pen and brown ink on oatmeal paper. 6⅜ x 8⅝ inches (168 x 219 mm.). Inscribed in graphite on verso by a modern hand: *RL West.* Watermark: 1805.

See above.

247

Landscape with Fortified Medieval City on a Cliff
1970.11:148

Pen and brown ink over black chalk. 4½ x 7¼ inches (114 x 185 mm.). Watermark: None.

This and the following drawing, which shows the same scenery with only slight variations, are perhaps sketchbook notations made by Raphael on a trip to Europe.

248

Landscape with Fortified Medieval City on a Cliff
1970.11:149

Black chalk. Two sheets of paper pasted together (one-third of the larger left blank). 8$\frac{15}{16}$ x 18$\frac{5}{16}$ inches (228 x 464 mm.) Numbered *53*. Watermark on larger sheet: 1813.

249

Large Tree with a Prostrate Nude Figure at Its Base
1970.11:50

Pen and brown ink, over black chalk. 13⅜ x 19⅞ inches (341 x 504 mm.). Watermark: None.

250

Moonlit Landscape
1970.11:109

Pen and black ink, black wash and white chalk on dark blue paper. 11½ x 12⅜ inches (292 x 315 mm.). Watermark: None.

The records of 1804 of the Royal Academy exhibitions include a picture by Benjamin West entitled *Moonlight* (no. 130) which, according to the quotation added by Graves (*op. cit.*, 4, p. 218), was inspired by Pope's Elegy: "What beckoning ghost along the moonlight shade Invites my steps," etc. Perhaps Raphael's romantic landscape in some way reflects his father's composition.

251

Gnarled Tree Trunk with Small Figures
1970.11:114 PLATE 125

Graphite. 7¾ x 11 inches (197 x 279 mm.). Watermark: Britannia.

It is suggested here that this attractive landscape drawing—so different in its painstaking, disciplined style from Raphael's impetuous and often rough manner—might be by the hand of his younger brother, Benjamin, Jr. The composition—a tree set prominently in the foreground of a flat landscape—the same wispy, leafless branches and tiny figures can also be found in *Bagshot Heath, Surrey*, one of a group of watercolor landscapes at the Boston Museum of Fine Arts (Acc. No. 42.584; 11 x 17½ inches. Fig. 63), which are attributed there to Benjamin, Sr., but do not quite fit into his known *oeuvre*. It is interesting to note that the same tree split by lightning and the same horse-drawn covered wagon appear in the drawing *Landscape with Brigands* attributed to Benjamin, Sr., at the Henry E. Huntington Library and Art Gallery, San Marino, California (Acc. No. 66.39; pen and ink on brown paper, 13¾ x 19⅝ inches. Fig. 64).

252

Group of Trees
1970.11:112

Brush and gray wash over traces of black chalk. 9 x 7¹⁄₁₆ inches (230 x 180 mm.). Watermark: Coat-of-arms with fleur-de-lis surmounted by crown.

The careful delineation of the tree trunks and branches and the parallel hatchings are similar to the technique used in the preceding drawing.

253

Nude Man Sitting at the Foot of a Tree
1970.1:41

Pen and brown ink. 6⅞ x 9⅜ inches (175 x 238 mm.). Watermark: None.

A similar subject, an old knotty tree with a small figure similarly posed but fully dressed, can be found in *Study of a Tree*, one of the early lithographs included in *Specimens of Polyautography*, 1803; the print is signed and dated *R. L. West 1802* (Frank L. Emanuel, "Some Sidelights on Early Lithography," *The Print Collector's Quarterly*, 21 (1934), p. 344, illus.; see also No. 54).

254

Landscape with Large Tree
1970.11:123

Graphite on heavy oatmeal paper (the mat from which the drawing discussed in entry 24 was removed). 14 x 15⁹⁄₁₆ inches (355 x 396 mm.). Watermark: None.

The same weatherbeaten forked tree with its

Fig. 64   Here attributed to BENJAMIN WEST, JR. Landscape with Brigands. *San Marino, California, Henry E. Huntington Library and Art Gallery.*

branches silhouetted against the sky found in the Boston watercolor landscape and the Huntington Library's drawing (Figs. 63, 64) can be seen in this rough sketch as well as in the tracing below (No. 255).

255

Landscape with Large Tree
1970.11:155

Graphite on brown tracing paper. 29⅛ x 20 inches (738 x 507 mm.). Watermark: None.

The composition of this large tracing is almost identical with that of the *Landscape with Brigands*, the drawing at the Henry E. Huntington Library and Art Gallery (Fig. 64); the three figures under the tree, the tree itself, the covered wagon, and the human skeleton at lower right appear in both. The tracing most likely was intended for transfer to the

lithographic stone. A related subject with three figures, perhaps a shepherd and two companions, under a large old tree is found in the lithograph signed *R. West* at the British Museum (1872-6-8-280; 9 x 12 inches. Fig. 65).

256

Rocky Peaks and Clouds
1970.11:174

Pen and dark brown ink on blue paper. 7⅜ x 10⅛ inches (192 x 256 mm.). Watermark: None.

257

Alpine Landscape with Eagle
1970.11:267

Pen and brown ink on two sheets of brown paper, now

Fig. 65 RAPHAEL WEST. Tree with Figures. Lithograph. *London, British Museum.*

joined. Part 1, Mountains, 6⅜ x 5¹⁄₁₆ inches (166 x 128 mm.); part 2, Eagle, 6⁷⁄₁₆ x 4¾ inches (164 x 121 mm.). Watermark: None.

258

Sheet of Sketches
1970.11:39

Black chalk on oatmeal paper. 10³⁄₁₆ x 12¹⁵⁄₁₆ inches (258 x 329 mm.). Seated figure on the right has been gone over with pen and black ink. Verso: Black chalk sketch of classical battle scene with warriors, chariot, and horses. Watermark: None.

259

Sketch of Gnarled Tree Trunk, and Face in Profile
1970.11:40

Pen and brown ink. 8 x 7¾ inches (203 x 197 mm.). Loss of lower left corner. Verso: Black chalk sketch of scene of execution. Watermark: Letters G R.

MISCELLANEOUS

260

Sheet of Sketches
1970.11:191

Brown and red tempera. 8¼ x 6 inches (210 x 152 mm.). Inscribed by the artist in pen and brown ink along left margin: *Starch – Resin – Musilage of Senigal – & sweet oil / in water –.* Verso: Pen and brown ink sketch, with some brushwork, of a nude male figure.

The three male heads in profile—verging on caricature—may well be the artist's trials in the medium, the ingredients of which are mentioned in the inscription.

261

Sketches of Beggars and Other Figures
1970.11:46

Pen and brown ink on gray paper. 12¾ x 7¾ inches (324 x 197 mm.). Horizontal crease in center. Stains of india ink. Verso: Graphite sketch of leg. Watermark: Crozier (close to Heawood 1210).

262

Figure Seated on Bank of River
1970.11:142

Pen and brown ink. 5¹³⁄₁₆ x 9¼ inches (147 x 235 mm.). Watermark: IV.

263

Mother and Child Seated at a Table
1970.11:259   PLATE 126

Pen and brown ink. 5½ x 5⅞ inches (140 x 151 mm.). Watermark: Letters J.B.

Could the young mother and her child in this charming domestic scene possibly be Mrs. Raphael West supervising the studies of her daughter Maria? The drawing *Mrs. West and Daughter Playing Catch* in the collection of Mr. and Mrs. Paul Mellon (pencil and ink, 7⅝ x 11¾ inches. Fig. 66) seems to support this assumption. Mrs. West's handsome appearance is known from the portrait *Mrs. West and Child* at the Dulwich College Picture Gallery (canvas, 36 x 27¾ inches) and her features in the painting seem to resemble those in the two drawings. A glowing description of her daughter at age fifteen—provided the young girl in the drawings really is Benjamin West's granddaughter Maria—can be found in William Dunlap's *History of the Rise and Progress of the Arts of Design in the United States* (in the chapter devoted to Raphael West, II, p. 291): Charles Robert Leslie and Washington Allston "were one day waiting in Mr. West's large painting room to see him, when the door opened, and a young girl of about fifteen came bounding in, but stopped suddenly on seeing strangers, blushed and ran out. We both thought

Fig. 66 RAPHAEL WEST. Mrs. West and Daughter Playing Catch. *Collection of Mr. and Mrs. Paul Mellon, Upperville, Virginia.*

we had never beheld anything so lovely. Mr. West entered soon after, and we asked him who the beautiful creature we had just seen was. He told us, she was his granddaughter, and added, 'She is a little Psyche'." Dunlap goes on to say that later on, when Maria herself had become a wife and mother, she sat to him for Anne Page in a Falstaff scene which he painted.

The following drawings are not by the hand of Benjamin or Raphael West. Since they were, however, part and parcel of the Morgan Library's group of drawings, they are included here.

SIR JAMES STEWART (1779–1849), fifth baronet of Allan Bank, Berwickshire

264

Cavalry Charge
1970.11:33

Pen and brown ink over graphite. 8⅜ x 13 inches (213 x 330 mm.). Inscribed in graphite: *Col. Stewart.* Watermark: 1810.

Sir James Stewart or Colonel Stewart, as he frequently signs his drawings and lithographs, was a spirited draughtsman specializing in battle scenes (see Iolo Aneurin Williams, *Early English Water-Colours*, London, 1952, p. 244). There is a lithograph signed *Col Stewart* of a similar subject showing cavalry charging into battle, at the British Museum (1874-7-11-1030; 6⅛ x 11¾ inches).

265

Design for Frieze with Mermaids, Tridents, and Putti
1970.11:153

Pen and brown ink over black chalk. 8 x 20⅞ inches (203 x 530 mm.). Squared for transfer. Inscribed in pen and brown ink: at upper left, $^{WH}_I$; on verso, Mr *Hamilton.* Watermark: None.

The name inscribed on the verso of this and the following drawing may refer to the artist or possibly a patron called Hamilton.

266

Two Designs for Ornament
1970.11:154

Pen and black ink over black chalk. 14⅜ x 14⅞ inches (365 x 379 mm.). Crease in center. Various inscriptions in pen and ink, mostly instructions and specifications concerning the execution of the design. Verso: Graphite sketch of the sculpture of an eagle on a base. Inscribed in pen and brown ink: Mr *Hamilton.* Watermark: None.

Plates

PLATE 1

one of the first attempts at historical composition by Benj. West, whilst in Philadelphia 1757

1   Rebecca at the Well

PLATE 2

2 Procession of Romans after the Ara Pacis, Rome

PLATE 3

6   The Infant St. John

PLATE 4

7   The Death of Epaminondas (?)

9   Hagar and Ishmael

PLATE 5

10   Thalia and a Male Nude

PLATE 6

19 Half-Draped Female Nude

13 St. Michael and the Dragon

PLATE 7

13ᵛ The Raising of Lazarus

15 The Raising of Lazarus

PLATE 8

16 Chryseis Returned to Her Father Chryses

PLATE 9

18   Sailing Vessel and Longboats

PLATE 10

20   Sketch for "The Death of the Earl of Chatham"

PLATE 11

21   Study for "The Crucifixion"

PLATE 12

23 Standing Male Figure and Other Sketches

PLATE 13

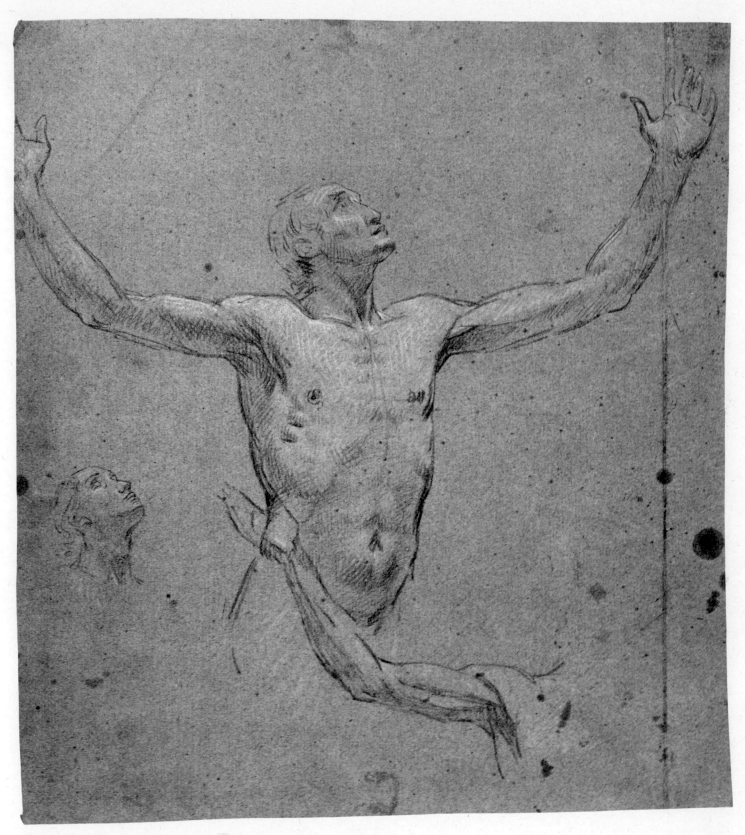

24   Male Figure with Arms Outstretched and Two Details

PLATE 14

22   Birth of Eve

PLATE 15

65   The Three Marys at the Sepulchre

PLATE 16

25 Agrippina with Her Children Going through the Roman Camp

25ᵛ Landscape with Hay Wagon

PLATE 17

26 The Resurrection

PLATE 18

27   The Risen Christ

PLATE 19

30   Three Studies for the Figure of Christ in a "Resurrection"

PLATE 20

31 Christ and the Angel

PLATE 21

32 The Temptation of Christ

PLATE 22

33   Esau Selling His Birthright for a Dish of Pottage

34   Esau Selling His Birthright for a Dish of Pottage

PLATE 23

38   Head of a Cavalier

37   Oliver Cromwell Pointing to the Mace

PLATE 24

39   Death on a Pale Horse

PLATE 25

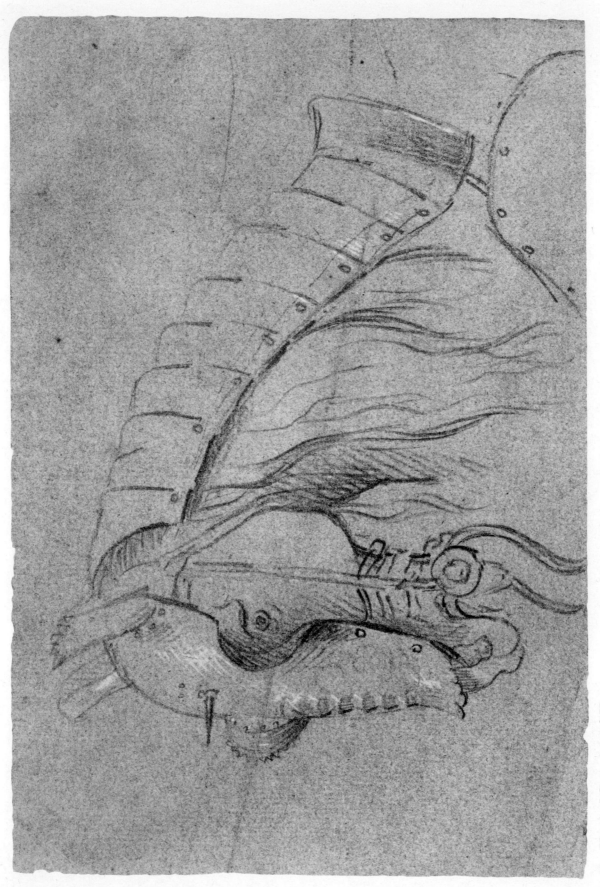

42   Head of Caparisoned Horse

PLATE 26

40   Seated Figure of Christ

PLATE 27

41   The Last Supper

PLATE 28

44   Costume Studies

PLATE 29

50   The Expulsion of Adam and Eve

PLATE 30

51   Moses Destroying Pharaoh and His Host in the Red Sea

PLATE 31

52   Aaron Staying the Plague

PLATE 32

54   Christ (Study for the Figure in "The Baptism")

PLATE 33

57　Rustic Lovers Struck by Lightning

PLATE 34

56   Harvesters near Windsor Castle

PLATE 35

1970. 11. 201

56ᵛ   Sketches of Landscape and Reaper

PLATE 36

58   The Toilet of Venus

PLATE 37

63 Sibyl

PLATE 38

59   The Angel in the Sun

PLATE 39

60   Sketches for Windows at Fonthill Abbey

PLATE 40

67   Belisarius Recognized by His Soldiers

PLATE 41

70   The Rider on the White Horse

PLATE 42

71   The Throne of God in Heaven and The Book Sealed with
     Seven Seals

PLATE 43

72   Sketch for a Last Judgment

PLATE 44

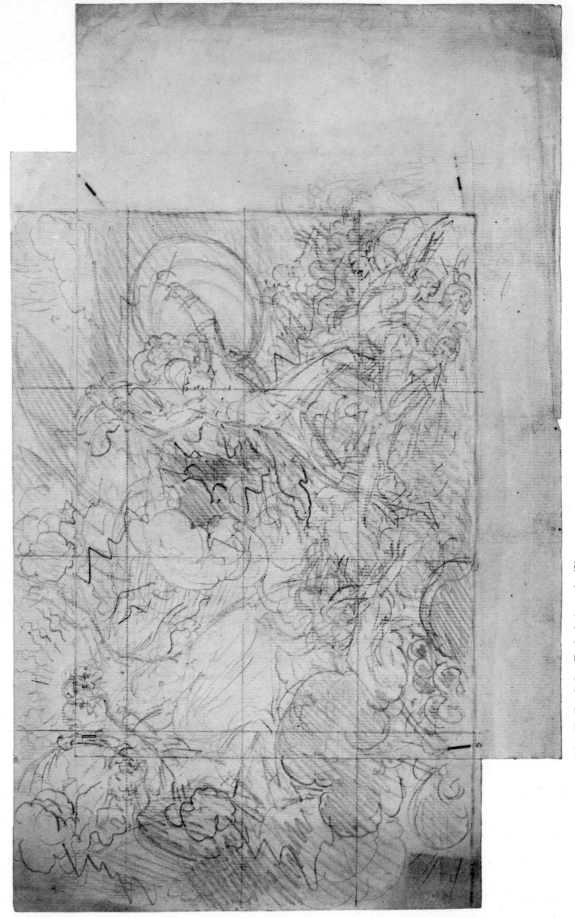

73   Fall of the Rebel Angels (?)

PLATE 45

74 Thetis Bringing the Armor to Achilles

PLATE 46

76 Thetis Bringing the Armor to Achilles

PLATE 47

76ᵛ   Thetis Bringing the Armor to Achilles

PLATE 48

75   Study for the Figure of Achilles

PLATE 49

78   Study for the Legs of Achilles

79   Study for the Right Leg and Drapery
       of Achilles

PLATE 50

80   Design for a Helmet

PLATE 51

85   Study for the Figure of Achilles

PLATE 52

82   Achilles Wearing the Armor Brought by Thetis

PLATE 53

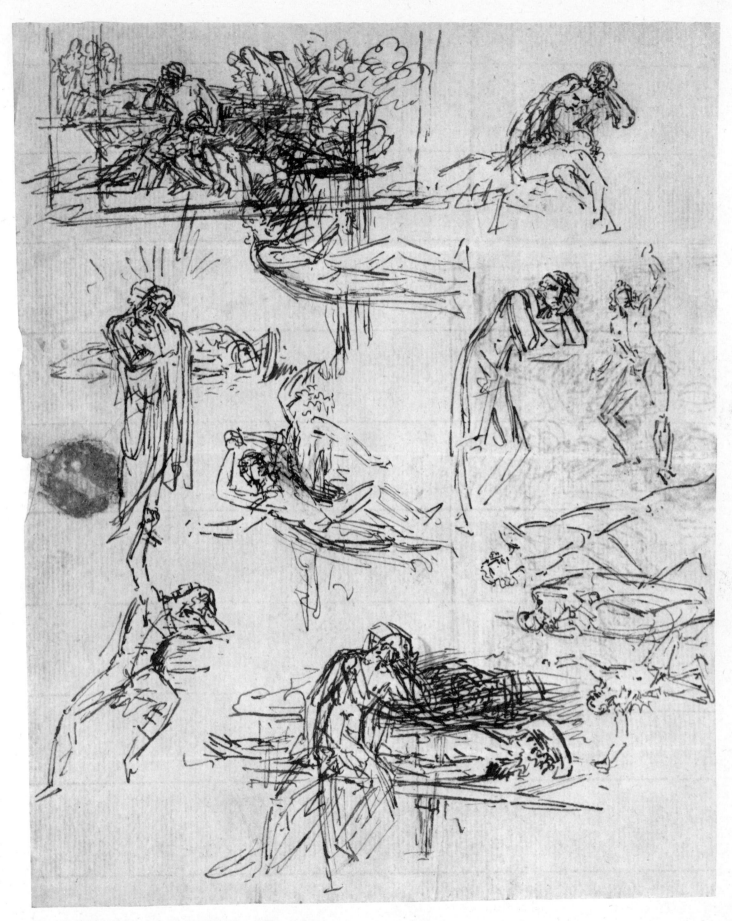

83   Achilles Mourning the Death of Patroclus

PLATE 54

5

84 Achilles Wearing the Armor Brought by Thetis

PLATE 55

86   Study for the Figure of Achilles

PLATE 56

81   Studies for the Figure of Achilles

PLATE 57

87 Midshipman's Berth and Cockpit Ladder of the "Victory"

PLATE 58

88   The Bard

PLATE 59

PLATE 60

91 Standing Nude Youth

PLATE 61

93   Allegory of Britannia

93ᵛ   Sketch for Allegory of Britannia

PLATE 62

94   Study for "Saul and the Witch of Endor"

PLATE 63

97 Christ Bound and a Group of Soldiers

96 Christ Bound

PLATE 64

99   Sketch for the Installation of "Christ Rejected by the Jews"

PLATE 65

103 Nude Youth with Drapery

102 The Victory of Waterloo

101 The Victory of Waterloo

PLATE 66

105v A Group of Witnesses of the Crucifixion

105 A Group of Witnesses of the Crucifixion

PLATE 67

PLATE 68

107 Peter's Denial of Christ

PLATE 69

108   Head of an Apostle

PLATE 70

113   Study of a Male Nude, Three-Quarter-Length

PLATE 71

113ᵛ   Study of a Male Nude, Full-Length

PLATE 72

115   Male Nude Seated on a Rock

PLATE 73

117 Male Nude Subduing a Serpent

PLATE 74

118 Standing Male Nude

PLATE 75

122　Seated Man and Torso

PLATE 76

119   Sketches of the Parthenon Metopes

PLATE 77

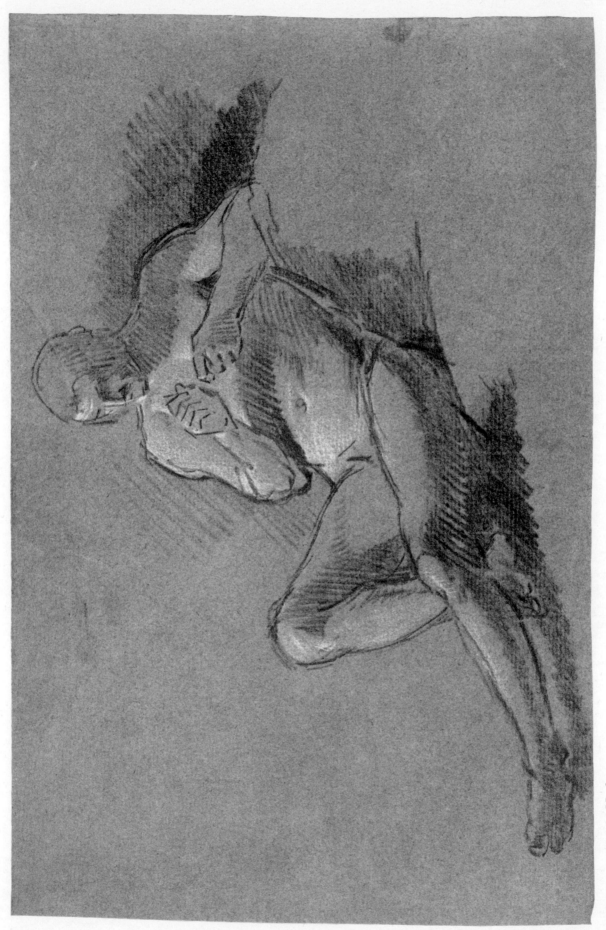

120 Seated Male Nude

PLATE 78

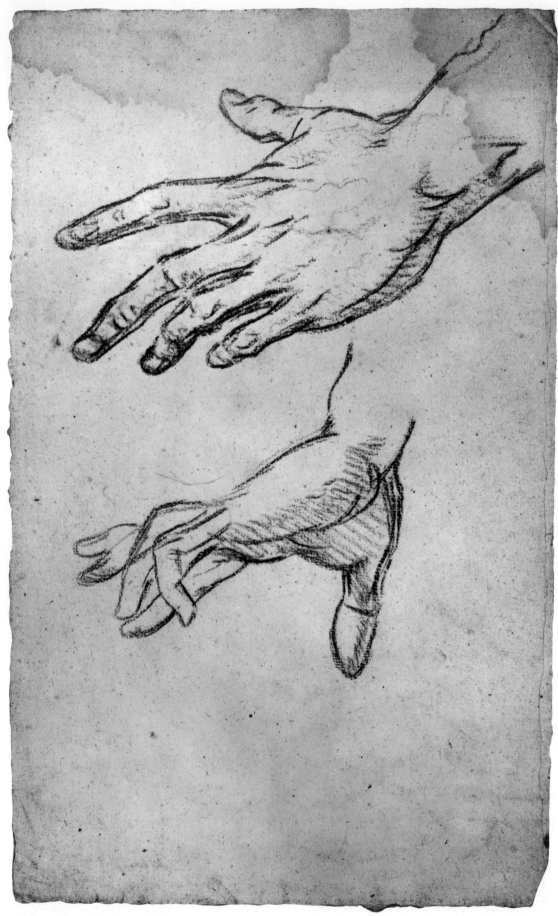

127^v   Two Studies of Hands

PLATE 79

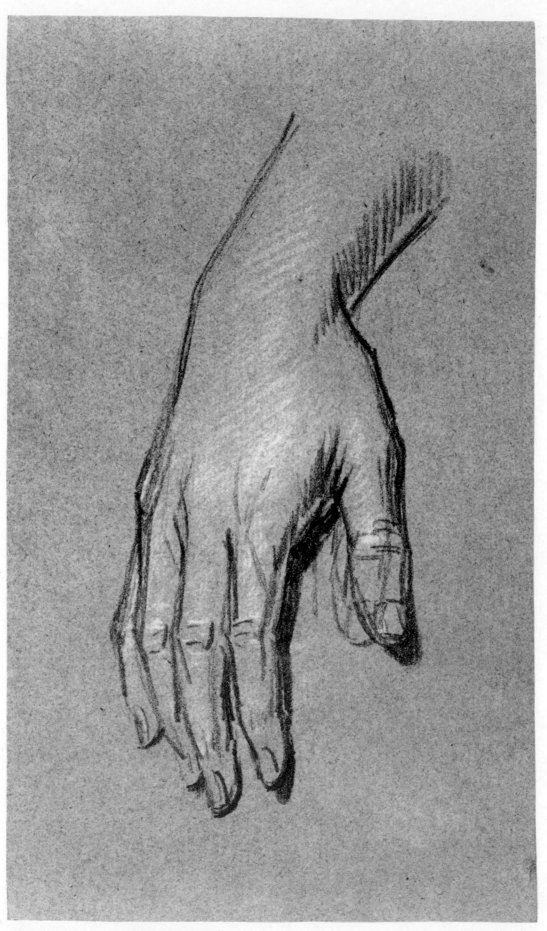

128 Study of a Woman's Hand

PLATE 80

141   Head of a Young Woman

154   Head of a Boy

PLATE 81

148   Soldier with Plumed Shako

148ᵛ   Sketch of Three Doves

PLATE 82

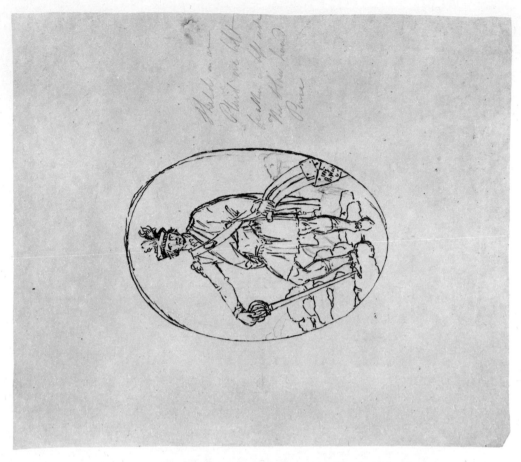

149 Man in Highland Dress

144 Sailor

PLATE 83

152   Family Group in Front of a House

PLATE 84

153   Portrait Head of a Lady

PLATE 85

155   Portrait of an Elderly Man with Long Hair

PLATE 86

158 Seated Woman with a Musical Instrument

PLATE 87

158ᵛ   Sketch for Seated Woman with a Musical Instrument

PLATE 88

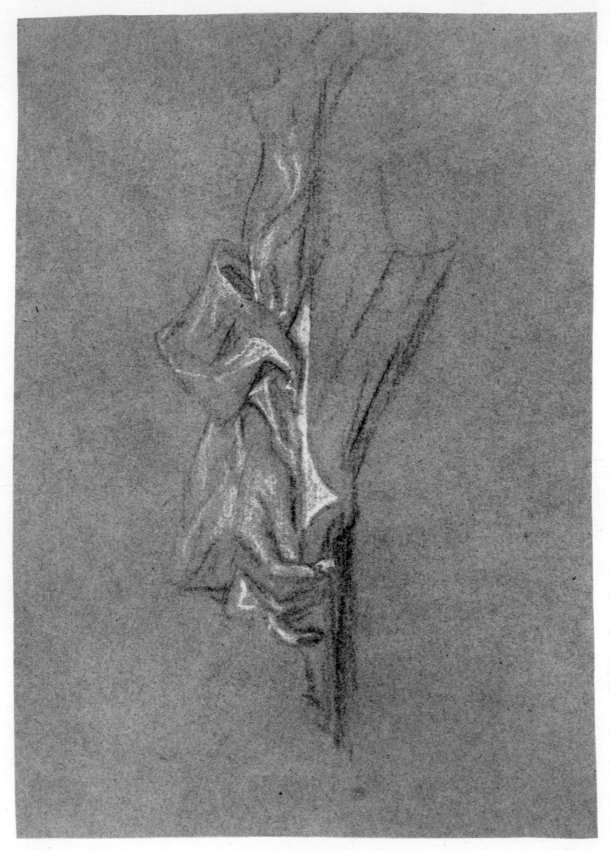

156   Hand in a Sleeve Holding Open Book

PLATE 89

161   Three-Quarter-Length Portrait of Napoleon

Bonaparte's Carriage – Drawn by Benj.ⁿ West

162   Bonaparte's Carriage

PLATE 90

168   Landscape with Two Men on Horseback

PLATE 91

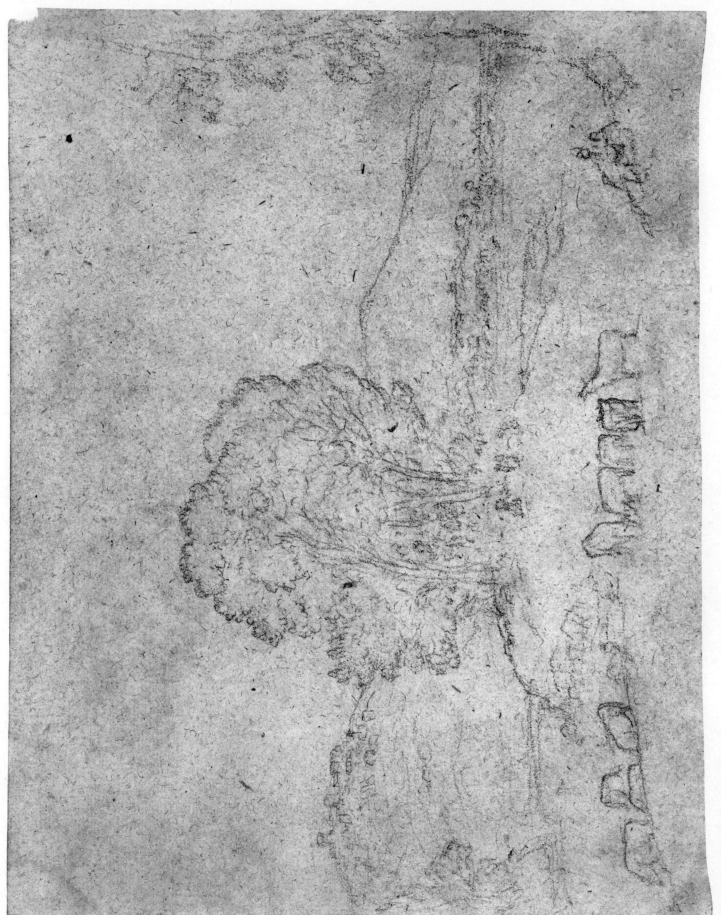

169 Landscape with Cattle

PLATE 92

171   Landscape with a Winding River

PLATE 93

172   Mountain Landscape with River and Building in Foreground

PLATE 94

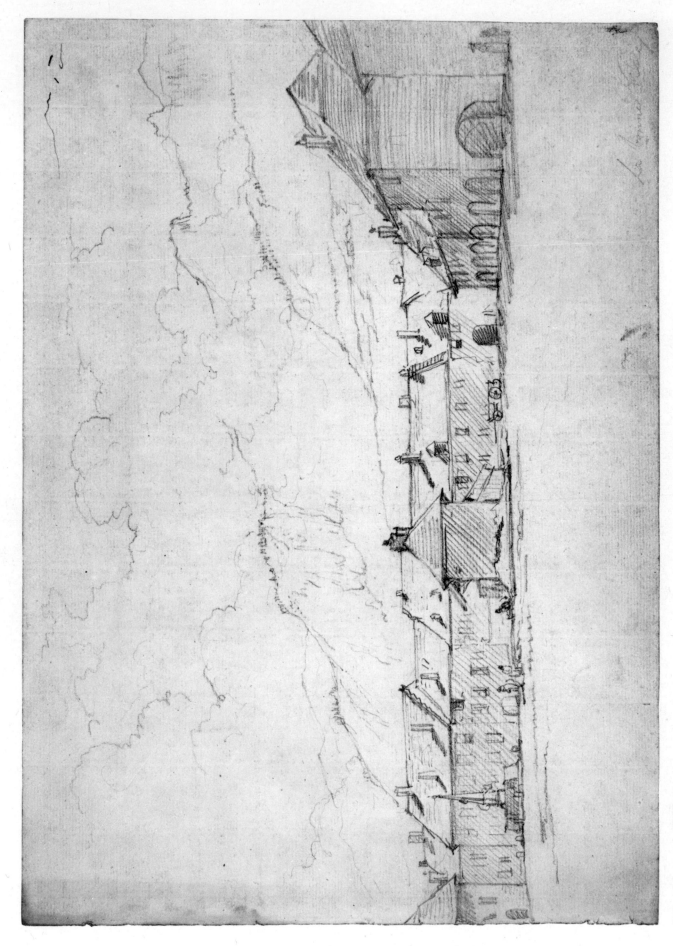

173   Mountain Village

PLATE 95

175 Trees in a Park

PLATE 96

174   Gnarled Tree Trunk

PLATE 97

176 Knotty, Gnarled Tree

PLATE 98

179 Landscape with Sheep at a Brook

PLATE 99

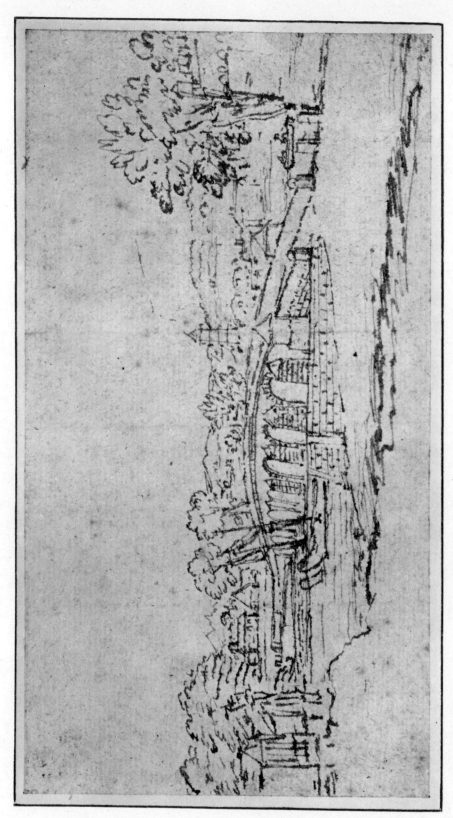

181   Kew Bridge with the Pagoda

PLATE 100

184   Weeping Rock on the River Wye

PLATE 101

183 View of Wrotham, Kent

PLATE 102

185   Landscape with Harvesting Peasants

PLATE 103

186   Landscape with a Lake and Farm Houses

PLATE 104

109   Stag Hunt

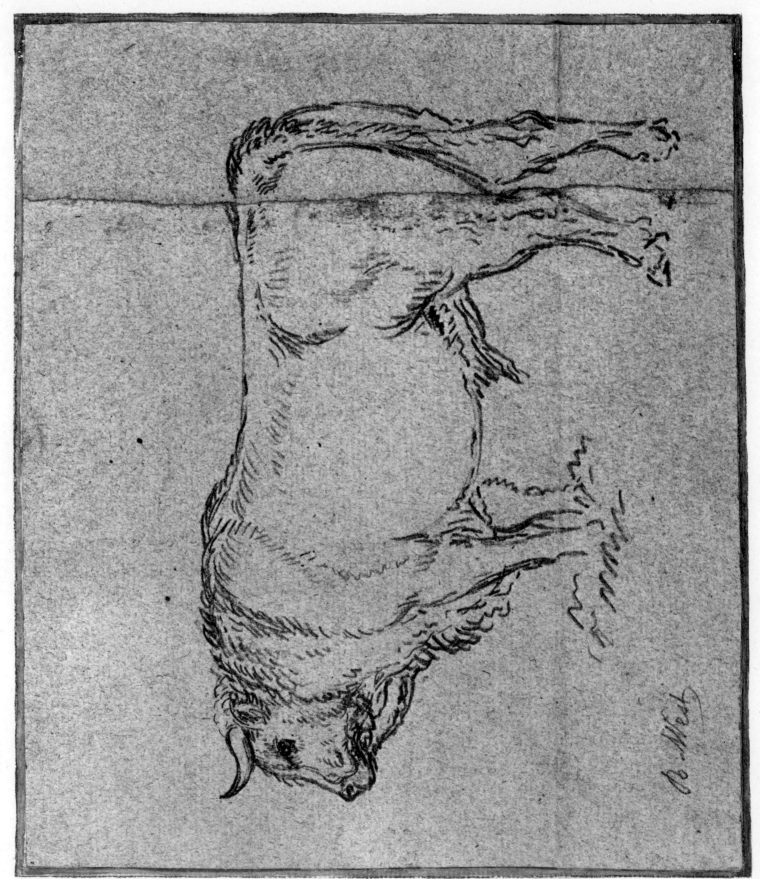

196   Sketch of a Bull

PLATE 105

PLATE 106

202   The Water-Bearer, after Raphael

PLATE 107

199   Michelangelo's Adam from the Creation of Eve, Sistine Chapel

PLATE 108

204 Alexander III, King of Scotland, Rescued from the Fury of a Stag by Colin Fitzgerald

PLATE 109

214 RAPHAEL WEST   Cadmus Slaying the Dragon

PLATE 110

215 RAPHAEL WEST Orlando Rescuing Oliver from the Lion

PLATE 111

216 RAPHAEL WEST Sketches for a Recumbent Figure

PLATE 112

217   RAPHAEL WEST   Brigand Lying under a Tree

PLATE 113

218 RAPHAEL WEST Brigand Lying under a Tree

PLATE 114

219 RAPHAEL WEST   The Creation of Eve (?)

PLATE 115

220   RAPHAEL WEST   Aeneas and the Cumaean Sibyl

221   RAPHAEL WEST   Sketch for "Macbeth" (Act I, Scene III)

PLATE 116

224 RAPHAEL WEST The Virgin and the Dead Christ

PLATE 117

225 RAPHAEL WEST St. Michael

PLATE 120

237   RAPHAEL WEST   View of the Town of Geneva on Seneca Lake

240   RAPHAEL WEST   Landscape with Log Cabins
near the Genesee River

PLATE 121

238   RAPHAEL WEST   The Hotel at the Catskill Mountains

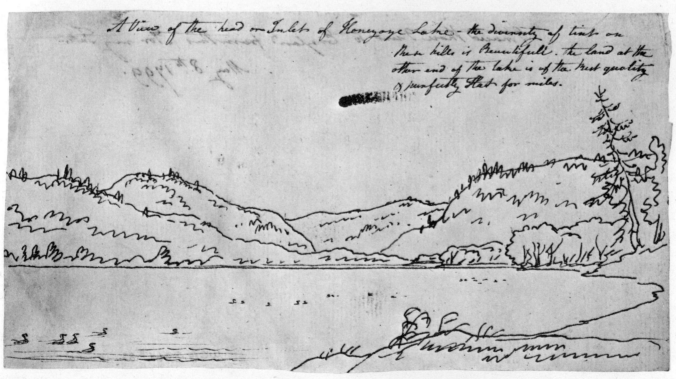

239   RAPHAEL WEST   View of Honeyoye Lake

PLATE 122

241 RAPHAEL WEST Landscape with Log Cabin, Farmer and Pig

242 RAPHAEL WEST Landscape with Farm House and Farmer near a Pond

PLATE 123

243 RAPHAEL WEST Landscape with Lake and Fallen Trees in the Foreground

PLATE 124

PLATE 125

251   BENJAMIN WEST, JR.   Gnarled Tree Trunk with Small Figures

PLATE 126

263   RAPHAEL WEST   Mother and Child Seated at a Table

Produced by
The Stinehour Press
and The Meriden Gravure Company